PRAISE FOR

STOP ACTING LIKE A CHRISTIAN, JUST BE ONE

Chris Caine is a unique voice to this generation. She is also one of the most readable writers I've read in a long time! This book won't just make you think—it will challenge you to change. It's a must-read for anyone who is serious about going to the next level spiritually!

Mark Batterson
Lead Pastor, National Community Church
Author, *In a Pit with a Lion on a Snowy Day*

Chris Caine has kicked Christianity up to the next level by returning to the radical purpose of new birth. If we are going to be authentic and relevant, we must embrace truth and allow it to transform us at our very core. This book will challenge every vantage and perspective you now hold while empowering you to walk in the truth and freedom you long for.

John and Lisa Bevere
Best-selling Authors/Speakers

Chris Caine is always real, radical and relevant. *Stop Acting Like a Christian, Just Be One* will inspire, equip and motivate you to *authentic* Christianity—which the world urgently needs.

J. John
Evangelist, Philo Trust
Chorleywood, Hertfordshire

I can't think of anyone more qualified to write this book than Christine Caine. She lives what she preaches! Christine's passionate about seeing people come into authentic relationship with Jesus, being transformed from the inside out and becoming soul-winners. I encourage you to take hold of the principles and lessons she shares from her hard-fought journey to freedom, and take up the challenge of being salt and light in your world.

Brian Houston
Senior Pastor, Hillsong Church
Sydney, Australia

This generation is desperately searching for something authentic. People are always watching us. They are watching to see if we are the real deal. Chris Caine shows us that without a transformed heart, we can never be the light that the world around us so desperately needs. Christine lives the message of this book, and I believe her passion for authentic Christianity will fuel your desire to stop acting and start *being*!"

Joyce Meyer
Best-selling Author and Bible Teacher

STOP ACTING LIKE A CHRISTIAN

JUST BE ONE

Christine Caine

Regal

From Gospel Light
Ventura, California, U.S.A.

Published by Regal Books
From Gospel Light
Ventura, California, U.S.A.
Printed in the U.S.A.

Regal Books is a ministry of Gospel Light, a Christian publisher dedicated to serving the local church. We believe God's vision for Gospel Light is to provide church leaders with biblical, user-friendly materials that will help them evangelize, disciple and minister to children, youth and families.

It is our prayer that this Regal book will help you discover biblical truth for your own life and help you meet the needs of others. May God richly bless you.

For a free catalog of resources from Regal Books/Gospel Light, please call your Christian supplier or contact us at 1-800-4-GOSPEL *or* www.regalbooks.com.

Library of Congress Cataloging-in-Publication Data
Caine, Christine.
  Stop acting like a Christian, just be one / Christine Caine.
    p. cm.
  ISBN-13: 978-0-8307-4373-5 (trade paper)
  1. Christian life. I. Title.
  BV4501.3.C335 2007
  248.4–dc22   2007012389

            1 2 3 4 5 6 7 8 9 10 / 10 09 08 07

Rights for publishing this book in other languages are contracted by Gospel Light Worldwide, the international nonprofit ministry of Gospel Light. Gospel Light Worldwide also provides publishing and technical assistance to international publishers dedicated to producing Sunday School and Vacation Bible School curricula and books in the languages of the world. For additional information, visit www.gospellightworldwide.org; write to Gospel Light Worldwide, P.O. Box 3875, Ventura, CA 93006; or send an e-mail to info@gospellightworldwide.org.

This book is dedicated to my beautiful daughter
Sophia Joyce Grace

CONTENTS

STOP ACTING LIKE A CHRISTIAN...

JUST BE ONE

STOP ACTING LIKE A CHRISTIAN...

LOVE THE LORD
YOUR GOD

I love being Greek, I thought to myself as I laced up my running shoes. *We're feisty, we're smart, and we heal quickly!* I couldn't believe how great I felt and that I was about to reacquaint myself with one of my favorite pastimes—running.

It had been way too long since I had worn these shoes, not that I had had any option about that the past several months. Even if I could have run during the last few months of my pregnancy, I certainly couldn't have squeezed my swollen feet into these shoes, let alone have been able to bend over and tie them. *It's going to be a great day!*

Now I only needed to wait for Lisa, my personal trainer, to arrive. It had only been a few weeks since I had given birth to my second beautiful daughter, Sophia Joyce, and although I had lost much of the "baby weight," I still had a few pounds to go and was ready to try to get rid of it. Today was my first training session with Lisa, and I was anxious to get moving. My plan was to have her develop an intense six-week fitness program that would get me back into my pre-pregnancy jeans.

If only the nurse from the labor and delivery floor could have seen me now. She wouldn't believe her eyes. I could still hear her voice echoing in my head: "Come on, Mrs. Caine, you need to wake up and get out of bed. If you don't do this today, your muscles will seize up and you'll be in even more pain than you are right now."

What do you mean more *pain?!* I had thought at the time. *Impossible!*

"We need to get you up and moving."

I almost laughed, but the fear of having to use my stomach muscles kept me silent. Besides, I knew she was right. This was my second C-section in just a few years, and I knew the importance of stretching and exercising the abdominal muscles right after the surgery. I must say that whoever came up with the old wives' tale about not remembering the pain of childbirth must have had some serious amnesia issues! For me, the not-so-fun aftermath of my first C-section was crystal clear in my mind—especially the piercing pain that came when I had tried to get out of bed for the first time after the delivery.

What you probably don't know about a C-section is that the process involves the slicing open of five layers of skin, tissue and lower stomach muscles in order to get to the baby. After the "peeling open" process (sorry if you're starting to feel queasy), everything is carefully stitched back together again. That's when the healing begins, a process that involves weeks of painful rehabilitation, lots of rest, minimal lifting—and did I mention painful rehab?

Still, this was my second time around, and I knew that there wasn't any point in dwelling on the pain. I also knew that if I didn't start the recovery process almost immediately, all those muscles would begin to heal incorrectly. The repercussions could affect me the rest of my life.

So with every ounce of willpower that I could muster—and the help of the nurse and my husband, Nick—I slowly (and I mean *slowly*) sat up, put my feet on the floor and began to shuffle around my room. Needless to say, it was not my most glamorous moment, but at least I had taken a few steps on the road toward recovery.

But now that was all behind me! Today I was going to meet my new personal trainer. She'd be impressed by my strategy to get back into those jeans, and before I knew it, I'd be back to running my usual five miles a day.

Lisa arrived right on time. Before she could take off her jacket, I presented her with my six-week fitness plan. Her response was certainly unexpected. She laughed. Thinking she hadn't understood my plan, I debated whether to repeat myself. However, after she stopped laughing, she pulled out a mat and told me to lie down on my back. I obediently followed her instructions, although I wondered why I was paying her to tell me to lie on my back when clearly I needed to get started with my workout.

Lisa then began to talk to me about my body's core. I have to admit that I never actually knew that my body had a core. I never liked science or anatomy classes in college, and at that point I couldn't have cared less about my "core." I just wanted to get back into my jeans . . . yesterday!

Considering I was paying her by the hour, I decided to hear her out. In great detail, she explained to me what my body had been put through over the last few weeks, specifically how the surgery had significantly weakened the core muscles of my body.

These core muscles connect all our limbs to our spine while literally holding our skeleton together—and they are responsible for every movement our body makes. This "core" needed to be strengthened before I took on any kind of strenuous activity, especially running. Lisa said I needed to throw out my plan, which focused on measurable, external success, and start a fitness program that was designed from the inside out. This would be the only way for me to avoid serious long-term muscular damage.

Lisa had me lie on the mat for 30 minutes of core muscle exercises. It seemed ridiculous, because I couldn't even feel anything (this reinforced my view that there was no such thing as a core—it was merely a figment of Lisa's imagination). To make matters worse, she informed me that these exercises were all I would be allowed to do for the next few weeks! Admittedly, as she was speaking I was working out the most scenic route for the jog I would be taking as soon as she left. But in the end, I decided to listen to her advice (after all, she was the professional) and give her fitness regime a try. During the next few weeks, that mat and I became very good friends as I spent time each day doing my core exercises.

It was during one of these seemingly "useless" sessions while lying flat on my back contracting and expanding, breathing in and breathing out, that I realized this whole "physical core" thing had a parallel in our spiritual lives. We not only have a physical core but a spiritual core as well. As I began to consider the concept of a spiritual core and the role it plays in our daily lives, I realized just how crucial it is. Just as our physical core is responsible for every move our body makes, our spiritual core is responsible for our every thought, emotion, reaction and decision. Just as I had to commit to doing exercises that would build my physical core, so too we have to be actively committed to developing and strengthening the muscles that are responsible for keeping our spiritual core strong.

Becoming Christlike

I had a measurable goal when it came to getting back in shape: to fit back into my "pre-baby" jeans. This was my motivation, and it helped keep me focused, even when my flesh wanted nothing more than to sleep in rather than exercise! Similarly, before we can get on with building our spiritual core, we need to understand what our target is and what it is we're aiming for. Quite simply, the goal of every Christian is to become more Christlike—after all, the very word "Christian" denotes "a Christ follower." Paul tells us, "Therefore be imitators of God as dear children" (Eph. 5:1). We should heed his exhortation and earnestly desire to be like Jesus in every way.

Paul also writes, "Imitate me, just as I also imitate Christ" (1 Cor. 11:1). When I think about this, I wonder exactly what Paul meant by "imitate." Does this mean that we should wear the same style toga and sandals that Jesus wore? Does this mean we should only eat kosher foods? Probably not. In fact, I think it is obvious that Paul is speaking about following Jesus' example in terms of His mission, values, motivation, priorities, thinking, teaching and attitude. In other words, being imitators of Christ is something that stems from the inner core of our being. This occurs when who we are on the inside begins to be transformed as we become more like Him and have His heart and mind. The internal change in turn is reflected in the way we speak, think and act.

The crucial component we need to understand is that imitating Christ begins with developing a strong spiritual core. If we simply try to imitate Christ's external behavior—being kind, compassionate and merciful without strengthening our spiritual core—then we risk missing out on the very process that makes us Christlike. Invariably, we end up acting like a Christian sometimes, but not truly being a Christian at all times.

Think about Jesus: His actions stemmed from who He was. The *doing* part flowed naturally from Jesus *being* authentically Jesus. This *being* stemmed from His spiritual core. In other words, Jesus did not try to act like anything He was not. Therefore, if we are to be imitators of Christ, we need to stop trying to *act* like Christians (external actions) and instead focus on *being* a Christian at our core (internal transformation). When this becomes our focus, we will discover that it's not difficult to act like a Christian, because we simply will be one. Period.

"Inside Out" Living

Many of us struggle with living each day as authentic followers of Christ. We don't understand why we seem to do okay for a week after hearing an inspirational message, but then fall back into old patterns of behavior before we know it. We keep trying to fix our behavior, promising wholeheartedly that we won't shout at the kids again, be rude to our spouse, react in traffic, lie, cheat, steal, gossip or gamble.

Invariably, we find ourselves unable to sustain our resolve— and we fail to control our actions (again!). As a result, we feel terrible about ourselves, vowing to never again shout at the kids, be rude to our spouse or react in traffic . . . you get the picture! This never-ending cycle causes many people to give up trying or, worse still, give up on God altogether. That's what happens when we try to live our Christian lives from the outside in instead of from the inside out. The tension between our inner world and outer world cannot be sustained long-term and will inevitably have a detrimental effect on our life.

All too often we compartmentalize our life and divide it into segments, which is where the confusion begins. We become actors, taking on the role of who we think we're supposed to *be* depending on our audience or our circumstances. For example, at church, we're *supposed to be* a Christian, so we *act* like one (some of us could win an Oscar for our performances). Around our Christian friends we're *supposed to be* a Christian, so we *act* like one. At work, we try to *act* like a Christian because we're *supposed to be* one, but there we don't have to play the role too well because our coworkers are not quite as familiar with the Christian "script."

When we go home, we act like our real selves, because we believe that our secret is safe with our family. Then the doorbell rings. It's amazing how quickly we can shift and play the part of the perfect life even if moments before our house was more like the perfect storm. We move the couch over three feet to cover the stain on the carpet, wipe the dust off the ceiling fan blades, threaten the kids with lifelong house arrest if they so much as look the wrong way, and yell at the dog. As soon as our guests arrive, we are instantly the model family.

Many of us do the very same thing with God. We can be on our way to church having a knockdown fight with our spouse, but as soon as we hit the parking lot, the "spirit of the visiting God" comes upon us. We smile at the greeters, using a very cordial tone of voice (the one we haven't used since last service), sing and worship with holy hands raised (the same ones we were thinking of using for a good thwack on the back of our husband's head just a moment ago) and play out our role as the perfect Christian for about two hours. We have a nice visit with God, and then we get back in the car and go back to acting like our real selves again.

This cycle continues because we have not allowed Jesus to permeate the very core of our being. True transformation hasn't occurred. We haven't really undergone conversion—just a partial behavior modification. Essentially, we become actors in a drama rather than pilgrims on a journey. We try to act like something we are supposed to *be*.

This is not how God wants us to live. Jesus doesn't want us to simply act like Christians. He wants us to authentically *be* Christians. But the only way for this to occur is by allowing Him to work on us from the inside out. God doesn't want to have a relationship with us from afar. No, He wants to be actively involved in every aspect of our life. *THE MESSAGE* puts it this way: "The Word became flesh and blood, and moved into the neighborhood" (John 1:14). I love the way Eugene Peterson interprets this Scripture, because this image makes it clear that God wants to be part of everything in our lives. He is not satisfied with merely having visitation rights every Sunday or Wednesday at a church service or two. He wants to be at the core of who we are and what we're becoming.

Looking the Part Isn't Enough

It was on the ski slopes in Australia that I experienced firsthand the consequences of trying to act like something that I wasn't. I had been invited to be the chaplain on a youth ski trip at a premier ski resort in Australia. Although I'd never skied before, I accepted the invitation. I asked a friend of mine who used to be a professional skier if I could borrow some of her stuff, and she let me borrow her very chic, top-of-the-line ski gear. She said, "Well, at least you'll look the part!"

As we got ready to leave on our trip, all the kids kept asking me if I'd ever skied before. Have you ever been in a situation in which you don't want to lie but you don't want to tell the truth either? Well, this was one of those times. I avoided answering the question by leaving to change into my ski outfit. When I got onto the bus, I could hear an audible gasp from everyone because I looked like a professional with my purple ski suit and all of my matching designer gear. It was a holy moment, and I looked fabulous!

When we got to the slopes, we were told ski lessons had been arranged for anyone who needed them. Clearly, I couldn't be bothered with that. How hard could this skiing thing be? You go up and then you come down, right?

I looked for the lift that went up to the highest peak and then got in line (I'm an all-or-nothing kind of girl, and at this point I didn't know what "Black Diamond" meant—it just looked pretty). There was a guy who was going to get on the lift with me, and apparently we were supposed to simultaneously jump up as the seat backed into us. I jumped, missed the T-bar lift and, predictably, it left without me.

After several failed attempts, I eventually figured out the T-bar thing and then held on for dear life as I ascended higher and higher, all the while wondering why they didn't supply oxygen masks on these things. I gracefully disembarked at the top (okay, I totally fell off) and then somehow managed to begin my descent (largely by keeping my eyes closed!). Suddenly, a chilling thought occurred to me: *How do I stop?*

Off in the distance, I saw a group of about nine children who were listening to an instructor give some valuable lessons about how to stop. I thought, *If I just get behind them and do what they are doing, I'll be okay. If they can do it, I can do it.* Obviously, I didn't factor in the speed at which I was approaching, because my entrance turned into a game of ten-pin bowling as I knocked down all the children—and the instructor! Thankfully, no one was hurt.

That's how I discovered a new technique of stopping on the slopes (I'm pretty sure they're going to use it at the next winter Olympics). It was quite a simple technique, really. Whenever I saw a tree, I'd hit it, and then I'd fall. If I saw a rock, I'd aim for it, and then I'd fall. I figured the Caine Stopping Technique was better than the Ten-Pin Bowling Technique. I soon became very familiar with every tree, rock and bush on that slope. Needless to say, my battered and bruised body began to take on the same hue as my purple ski suit!

It was very apparent on the slopes that day that although I looked great on the outside and had all the best gear at my disposal, it had no bearing on my performance as an actual skier. I didn't have any of the knowledge, skill, experience or strength on the inside of me that a real professional skier needs to have. In the end, looking the part counted for nothing!

The same holds true for us as Christians. We can look the part by having the best gear in hand (our Bibles, our WWJD amulets, our fish bumper stickers); by refraining from certain behaviors such as smoking, drinking or cussing; or by going to church and singing in the choir. We certainly can be perceived as a successful Christian by looking the right way, having the right "accessories" and acting the right way. But if all of this does not stem from who we really *are* at our core, our faith is really just a sham.

We are supposed to be transformed into the image of Jesus. If we reject the transforming grace of Christ, then we are just like the Pharisees Jesus describes in the book of Matthew:

> Woe to you, scribes and Pharisees, hypocrites! For you are like whitewashed tombs which indeed appear beautiful outwardly, but inside are full of dead men's bones and all uncleanness. Even so you also outwardly appear righteous to men, but inside you are full of hypocrisy and lawlessness (23:27-28).

The fact is that Jesus despises hypocrisy. He wants authentic followers. He wants us to be able to echo the words of Paul: "But we all, with unveiled face, beholding as in a mirror the glory of the Lord, are being transformed into the same image from glory to glory, just as by the Spirit of the Lord" (2 Cor. 3:18). Remember, it's not about the Jesus sandals—it's about the Jesus core!

Unfortunately for our flesh, which craves instant results, this transformation is not something that happens overnight. That would be like my believing that prayer alone would get me back into my pre-Sophia jeans—and believe me, I tried!

We have to be willing to work at it. We cannot allow ourselves to be sidetracked by the external quick-fix plan. Instead, we must be committed to strengthening our spiritual core, which is all about an internal work that brings about our transformation into the image of Christ.

If our goal is to truly be like Christ (which I know yours is, or you wouldn't have this book in your hands right now), then we're not focused on *doing* Christianity but rather on *being* Christians. The natural byproduct is that we will end up doing what Christians are supposed to do. This removes all of the striving from our Christian journey because we no longer have to try to *act* like a Christian. We can simply be one.

Heart, Soul and Mind

"So, what exactly is this 'spiritual core'?" I hear you ask. As we journey though this book together, we will discover that our spiritual core muscles are described in the Great Commandment. Jesus said, "'You shall love the LORD your God with all your heart, with all your soul, and with all your mind.' This is the first and great commandment. And the second is like it: 'You shall love your neighbor as yourself'" (Matt. 22:37-39). From this commandment, we can see that our spiritual core muscles are our heart, soul and mind. These are what enable us to love God wholly and completely.

In order to have the capacity to fulfill the Great Commandment in our lives, we must first learn how to effectively exercise our heart, soul and mind muscles. Just as our physical muscles are connected, giving us the ability to stand, walk, sit and run, our heart, soul and mind are also interrelated. We must develop all of our core spiritual muscles if we are to be spiritually healthy.

Let me explain it this way: A body builder wouldn't go to the gym week in and week out and only focus on building his biceps. He knows that without an exercise routine that develops his body as a whole—not just his biceps—his other muscles would atrophy and eventually become useless. Similarly, we have to focus on strengthening and growing all three muscles that make up our spiritual core—or we risk growing stagnant, complacent and lukewarm, which would hinder all God wants to do in and through us.

Strengthening our spiritual core is not just for our benefit—it's also for the benefit of others. Remember, God has called us to love Him and to love others. Therefore, we must focus on developing each of these muscles, because only then will we have the capacity to not only love God but to also see ourselves as God sees us. This is crucial, because if we are commanded to love our neighbor as we love ourselves, then it is imperative that we actually love, value and esteem ourselves. If we truly love God with all of our heart, soul and mind, then we also truly love ourselves for whom God has made us to be and are able to love others for whom He has made them to be. We will always love our neighbor as we love ourselves. For this reason, it is crucial that we have the right perspective of ourselves. It's from this place of authentic relationship with God that we can love our neighbor as ourselves.

WITH ALL YOUR HEART

The day was absolutely perfect! The sanctuary was beautifully decorated, almost a dreamlike vision, as I walked down the lily-laced aisle in my enormous wedding dress (seriously, even as I was carefully balancing inside all the hoops and yards of fabric I had no idea how I made it through the door). Nick was at the end, looking smashing in his tux, with a smile from ear to ear.

As I made my way down the aisle, with all of my friends and family there to share my big day, I could hear my Greek mother crying tears of relief that her only daughter was *finally* getting married. The entire service then went as rehearsed, and we came to the culmination of the ceremony—the wedding vows. I was very excited, because I had planned a surprise.

Nick went first. I could see a few tears in his eyes as he said his vows to me. I was really glad about the tears because as he looked through them, I knew they made me look soft and feminine, just like in those old black and white movies where the heroine always looked perfect through a soft filter on the camera lens. I wanted Nick to remember me looking like that. He recited his vows, and then it was my turn.

When the pastor asked me to repeat after him, I announced to everyone that I had written my own vows and was ready to deliver them to my wonderful Nick. He was surprised—and a bit intrigued. I cleared my throat and began: "I, Christine, take you, Nick, to be my husband, my partner in life and my one true love. I will be faithful to you forever and ever, unless someone better comes along. *[What? Did I just say that out loud?!]* I will be yours in time of prosperity, but I'm not sure I will hang around if you don't keep bringing home that fat check of yours. *[What was happening?! I tried to stop talking, but my mouth had taken over.]* I will gladly respect and submit to you as long as you always do things my way, and I will cherish you in old age as long as you continue to work out, because I do not want you to break a hip or anything. *[This is not what I rehearsed!]*"

Shock spread through the whole place as Nick quietly stood there looking at me with a bewildered expression on his face. I could hear my mother crying hysterically, hiccups and all. I had ruined everything!

I shot up in bed and gasped for air. My eyes darted over to the clock, which read 5:47 A.M. *Oh, thank You, God! It was all just a dream!* It was still only the morning of my wedding day. I breathed a sigh of relief and began to laugh at the craziness of such a dream. Even though it had seemed frighteningly real, I knew it had nothing to do with reality. I got out of bed and began to get ready for what was going to be one of the most beautiful days of my life.

When Nick and I exchanged our wedding vows (for real, not at all like my dream), we committed 100 percent of our hearts to one another. If we had entered our marriage only halfheartedly, we would have set ourselves up for inevitable failure. We knew that the only way to make our marriage work was to invest our *whole heart* in it.

The Bible teaches us that we, the Church, are the Bride of Christ. Paul writes, "For I am jealous for you with godly jealousy. For I have betrothed you to one husband, that I may present you as a chaste virgin to Christ" (2 Cor. 11:2). In the same way that a husband desires complete devotion from his bride, God requires our complete commitment, passion, faithfulness and fidelity. He wants a relationship with us that is heartfelt, spontaneous, vibrant, alive and reciprocal.

In a healthy marriage, neither person wants the other to begrudgingly fulfill his or her marriage obligations out of guilt, condemnation or force but rather from a genuine heart commitment, conviction and desire. If the husband or wife is merely going through the motions of being married, the marriage becomes nothing more than an empty, boring and passionless living arrangement. The two people involved in this union are simply *acting* like a married couple rather than enjoying the benefits of truly *being* married.

It is little wonder that the Great Commandment begins with loving the Lord our God first and foremost with all our heart. He longs for authentic relationship with His Bride, not a mere religious obligation or empty ritual. The prophet Isaiah recounts God's words: "These people draw near with their mouths and honor Me with their lips, but have removed their hearts far from Me, and their fear toward Me is taught by the commandment of men" (Isa. 29:13). It is evident from this Scripture that God is not at all impressed by empty words or heartless platitudes. In fact, it makes Him angry when our words and actions are not sincere.

We must take care that our Christianity does not become mere lip service or hollow actions. God wants a genuine relationship that stems from our heart.

We should never make the mistake of thinking that we can fool God with our spiritual acts. God always looks beyond what man can see to the condition of the human heart. We see this clearly when God said to Samuel, "Do not look at his appearance or at his physical stature, because I have refused him. For the LORD does not see as man sees; for man looks at the outward appearance, but the Lord looks at the heart" (1 Sam. 16:7).

When we embrace God and His purpose wholeheartedly, it is easier to stay passionate about our faith, our spiritual disciplines and every other aspect of our spiritual walk. All of our actions and activities flow from our love relationship with God rather than from an obligation to fulfill a Christian requirement. We possess a love for others, for church, for reading our Bibles, for praying and for giving and serving. We love what God loves and desire to do what He does; it is the natural outflow of our heart.

Because love is so important, we must ensure that we continually strengthen our heart, this core spiritual muscle. We can do this by spending quality time with God, staying in close communication with Him and remaining obedient to His Word. It is through an intimate and daily relationship with God that we are able to give Him our whole heart.

Passion Is Not an Obligation

I remember a time before Nick and I started dating when he found out from a friend of mine that I swam at the local swimming pool at 6 A.M. each morning. I had been doing these early morning swims for almost a year, and up to that point I had never seen Nick at the pool. All of a sudden, I began seeing him there each morning, already in the pool and doing laps by the time I got there. There is nothing pleasant about doing laps at daybreak—the water is cold and getting out is even colder! But alas, Nick was not deterred. He was in love and on a mission.

After about a week, we "accidentally" (actually a well-planned accident on Nick's part) bumped into each other, and I asked him what he was doing at the pool so early in the morning. He looked at me indignantly and exclaimed, "What do you mean? I'm always here at this time. I love swimming this early!" Of course, only later were my suspicions confirmed that the sole purpose of Nick's being at the pool so early was to get my attention. No one had to convince Nick to do it, because he had a passion for a petite Greek woman and he was going to do whatever it took to take home his prize! And his passionate affection won the day—we eventually were married.

When we are in love, we will do anything to be with the person who has captured our heart. In fact, we not only long to be with them but also would literally do anything for them. Many of us begin our relationship with God like this. Overwhelmed with a revelation of His love, grace and mercy, there is nothing that we wouldn't do to try to please Him. Our earnest desire is to be with Him and become like Him.

Yet it is only by continually strengthening our spiritual heart muscle that we will be able to sustain this kind of passionate commitment to God for the duration of our Christian walk. In the same way that a natural relationship left alone will just fizzle out and eventually die, so too will our relationship with God.

In order to ensure that our love for God will not grow cold, we must proactively "keep [our] heart with all diligence, for out of it spring the issues of life" (Prov. 4:23). If we do not guard this core muscle, it will begin to weaken, and the very things that we once did wholeheartedly will eventually become nothing more than religious burdens. We will begin to think thoughts like, *Do I have to go to this church service? Can I really afford to give this offering? Why can't they get someone else to volunteer?* Or we may never think these thoughts but just mindlessly go through the motions of acting like a Christian without truly being one from our heart.

In the book of Revelation, Jesus rebuked the Ephesian church for leaving their first love—Him—and settling for Christian activity. Although they were fulfilling all of the external requirements of Christianity, they were missing something fundamental. They no longer loved God with their whole heart. Jesus said to them:

> I know your works, your labor, your patience, and that you cannot bear those who are evil. And you have tested those who say they are apostles and are not, and have found them liars; and you have persevered and have patience, and have labored for My name's sake and have not become weary. Nevertheless I have this against you, that you have left your first love (Rev. 2:2-4).

It was crucial that Jesus addressed this issue with the Ephesian church so that they would not become hard and legalistic, full of empty rituals and obligation. These would ultimately lead to a dead, empty church, a far cry from what Jesus intended. If we want the life of God to flow freely within our hearts, we must never allow anything to hinder the passion that we have for the Lord and His people. I was recently reminded how one small blockage could have profound ramifications.

It was my fortieth birthday party, and my family and friends were celebrating with me at my favorite Greek restaurant. We were partying in true Greek style: dancing to loud music, everyone talking at once (in more than one language, mind you), laughter erupting everywhere, and plates being smashed left and right.

"Nick!" I yelled in an effort to be heard over the music. "I'm going over to see my family!"

"What?!" he yelled back.

"I'm going over to see my family!"

Looking at me with a puzzled expression, he replied, "You're going to speak in a nunnery?!"

I laughed and repeated myself like tourists do when they are trying to communicate with the locals in a foreign country. After the second attempt, he finally understood what I was saying.

I walked over to chat with my family, thinking how blessed I was to have a life filled with so many special people. As I was speaking with my relatives, sharing laughs while dodging the flying plates, I noticed my uncle saying something to my mum. He was complaining about having some discomfort in his chest. He did look pale, but we assumed that it was a result of his having to climb the many stairs to the restaurant. He reassured us that the pain wasn't very serious, so at his urging we didn't really give it another thought.

The next day, I found out that when my uncle went home that night, the pain had grown worse and he had been rushed to hospital in an ambulance. He had suffered a heart attack. He underwent an eight-hour surgery, and the doctors told us that had my uncle not come into the hospital when he did, he probably would have died.

My uncle's heart had been damaged from years of poor diet, smoking and lack of exercise. The heart attack was caused by a blockage in one of the arteries that supplied blood to his heart. This was a wake-up call to our entire family and a sobering reminder of how important it is to have a healthy heart. It only takes one small blockage to cause a physical heart attack. The same is also true of the spiritual heart.

If we fail to care for our spiritual heart and neglect its health, we will never possess the spiritual strength we need to love God with all our heart. Jesus taught us, "The thief does not come except to steal, and to kill, and to destroy. I have come that they may have life, and that they may have it more abundantly" (John 10:10). By guarding our heart, we ensure that the enemy has no access to it and is therefore unable to steal the abundant life that Jesus came to give us.

Potential Heart Blockages

Unhealthy habits can often account for the breakdown of our physical bodies. For example, the more common causes of a physical heart attack are stress, a high-fat diet, lack of exercise, smoking and high blood pressure. To avoid having a heart attack, it stands to reason that we should eat a low-fat diet, exercise, not smoke and avoid situations that cause stress. By eliminating the potentially harmful behavior patterns that lead to blockages in our arteries, we can prevent a heart attack from ever happening. The best cure is prevention.

The same is true in our spiritual lives. We cannot ignore those things that cause a blockage in our spiritual heart muscle. Lack of spiritual health can cause us to leave our first love, which will eventually lead to a spiritual heart attack. Once we suffer such a heart attack, we find that our heart no longer beats passionately for God or His purposes. Instead, we substitute formalism for faith and empty ritual for the life of the Spirit.

In essence, by just going through the religious motions, we plug ourselves into an artificial life-support system. We mistakenly think we are alive, but in reality we are only existing. If we disconnected the wires from our empty rituals, there would actually be a spiritual flat line and no evidence of the life of God flowing in and through us. We were never created to settle for mere religion. Jesus did not die so that we could have a religious belief system but rather a life-giving relationship with our Father. God does not want us to spend our lives acting like a Christian. He wants us to be one from the inside out!

Of course, if we are to guard our hearts against potential blockages, it is important that we first identify what those blockages are. I believe that as Christians we all possess a sincere desire to love God with all our heart, yet we often unknowingly allow little things to build up inside of us. Slowly, these small subtle obstructions form very large blockages, which over a period of time clog our spiritual arteries and harden our heart by depriving it of access to its life source. We must do whatever it takes to ensure that these have no place in our lives as followers of Jesus.

Boredom

The first potential blockage we must all guard our hearts against is the *boredom blockage*. Married people often cite boredom as the reason that they have an affair. When people first get married, everything is an exciting, new adventure. However, if the couple does not commit to developing their marriage so that it will flourish, it soon becomes little more than a boring routine and an obligation. It is not surprising, then, that when boredom takes over a relationship, the husband and wife begin to look elsewhere for excitement and fulfillment.

Christians often leave their first love, Jesus, because they have allowed their faith to become a boring ritual rather than a breathtakingly intimate relationship with Him. When our Christianity has no life, no passion, it becomes dull, tedious, legalistic and mundane. As a result, our spiritual heart muscle is weakened to the extent that we no longer love the Lord our God with *all* our heart and we begin to pursue other avenues in our search for fulfillment and satisfaction.

We must remain bold and adventurous on the faith journey if we want to keep our relationship with God fresh and dynamic. We must never think that we have arrived, for the moment that we do this, we become stagnant and complacent. Instead, we must always fervently seek after the heart of God.

I love the passion and determination of the apostle Paul, who chose to never settle in any area of his life, especially in his relationship with God. He wrote:

> Not that I have already attained, or am already perfected; but I press on, that I may lay hold of that for which

Christ Jesus has also laid hold of me. Brethren, I do not
count myself to have apprehended; but one thing I do,
forgetting those things which are behind and reaching
forward to those things which are ahead, I press toward
the goal for the prize of the upward call of God in Christ
Jesus (Phil. 3:12-14).

Like Paul, we must commit to continually stretching our
heart muscle so that we may know Him more intimately. We do
this by seeking our Lord in His Word—and not just when we are
having a crisis, but on a daily basis. We also keep our heart strong
when we make it a priority to go to the Lord in prayer, asking for
His help, His grace and His heart for others.

Familiarity

The second potential blockage is the *familiarity blockage*. In a
marriage, if we are not careful, it is easy to become so familiar
with each other that eventually we take one another for granted.
The very things that were once appealing, endearing and cute
become contentious issues when too much familiarity creeps
into the marriage. In the same way, when the Christian walk
becomes familiar to us, we begin to take our relationship with
the Father for granted. Our hearts become sluggish, and the life-
flow of God's grace in our hearts begins to weaken and slow.

If we are to build a strong spiritual heart muscle and continue to love and serve God with passion, we must vehemently
guard our hearts against the familiarity blockage. Familiarity can
weaken our heart by causing us to take for granted many things
that were once fresh and exhilarating—things like reading our

Bible, listening to sermons and having access to Christian music, study materials and great churches. It can even cause us to become blasé about miracles, signs and wonders because they have become everyday events.

To keep our hearts alive and vibrant, we need to maintain an attitude of gratitude and thanksgiving. As Paul says, we must, "Thank [God] in everything [no matter what the circumstances may be, be thankful and give thanks], for this is the will of God for you [who are] in Christ Jesus [the Revealer and Mediator of that will]" (1 Thess. 5:18, *AMP*). Loving God with all our heart flows from a heartfelt gratitude to God for who He is and all that He has done and continues to do. When we remind ourselves of the fact that we owe Him everything, including our very being, we live in awe of Him and never run the risk of taking Him for granted.

Lust

The third potential blockage that will weaken and eventually destroy our spiritual heart muscle is the *lust blockage*. This is one of the main reasons why affairs happen, and it is also one of the very things that can cause us to leave our first love, the Lord.

Lust is when we have a desire for something that is not ours to have. Although we may be acting like "good" Christians on the surface, in our heart of hearts we may secretly be lusting after a particular ministry, position, title, partner, money, promotion, gift or talent. If we take our focus off God and His will for our life, our heart begins to seek after false loves.

In order to avoid this blockage from occurring, we must choose to fix our eyes on Jesus, who is the author and finisher of our faith. Our hearts must be set on Him and His plan and purpose for our lives. No other person or thing will satisfy us in the same way. Jesus said that we must "seek first the kingdom of God and His righteousness, and all these things shall be added to [us]" (Matt. 6:33). If we seek first the kingdom of God, He will add into our lives all other necessities and desires that align with His will.

Our spiritual heart muscle is weakened when we begin to pursue things above God and the blessings over the Blesser. In order to remain strong and healthy, God Himself must always be the object of our affection.

Laziness

The fourth potential blockage to our spiritual heart muscle is the *laziness blockage*. Many marriages fall apart simply because one or both of the marriage partners is too lazy to put in the work and effort that is required to build a healthy, strong marriage. A life-long union of love, fidelity, faithfulness, commitment, passion and loyalty does not happen on its own (just ask any married couple); it takes a lot of hard work. In the same way, as the Bride of Christ we need to understand that if we do not proactively and daily choose to love God with our whole heart and then act accordingly, our spiritual heart muscle will weaken.

A true sign that we are guarding our heart against spiritual laziness is that we continue to be about the Father's business, engaging our lives in the cause of Christ. Paul exhorts us to "be steadfast, immovable, always abounding in the work of the Lord, knowing that your labor is not in vain in the Lord" (1 Cor. 15:58). The fact that Paul uses the words "work" and "labor" in this passage indicates that these are essential components of the Christian life. God has a plan for each one of us, and we must do our part to see that plan realized.

Our goal is to ensure that these works, and the labor involved in bringing them to fruition, do not come from a sense of a religious obligation but flow from a passionate heart that is compelled to be about the Father's business. It is only then that we understand that the good works for which we have been created are not empty and dead works but life-giving ones that are full of purpose. The only thing that distinguishes religious obligation from good works is our heart attitude. When our hearts are full of zeal for the Lord, even the most mundane good works are deeply fulfilling.

Disobedience

The final potential blockage that can paralyze a thriving spiritual heart muscle is the *disobedience blockage*. In the same way that the refusal of a husband and wife to submit to each other in love can deaden the life of their marriage, so too our refusal to obey the Lord's leading can create a barrier between His love and our life. It is crucial that we understand the importance of our obedience even in seemingly insignificant and small things, because the truth is that every decision does matter to God. Every single day, we take steps toward fulfilling our spiritual destinies simply by choosing to hear and obey the voice of God and His Word.

If God instructs us to do something, either through His Word, a prompting in our heart or the words of a godly advisor, we must quickly obey. If we are not obedient to the last thing

God asked us to do, we cannot expect to be entrusted with more. Obedience may be something as simple as sending someone a note of encouragement, apologizing to a friend for being short tempered, volunteering in our church or going on a missions trip. Whatever it is, we must remember that every small step of obedience has eternal ramifications. If we choose not to obey, our hearts can begin to harden, which will inevitably silence the voice of God in our lives.

Many times the life of God disappears from our Christian walk because we postpone our obedience by filling our lives with distractions or religious activity. The Bible clearly teaches us that God wants our obedience above sacrifice. "Has the Lord as great delight in burnt offerings and sacrifices, as in obeying the voice of the Lord? Behold, to obey is better than sacrifice, and to heed than the fat of rams" (1 Sam. 15:22).

A New Heart

Having read this list of potential blockages, you may be thinking that you are a candidate for an all-out spiritual cardiac arrest. The good news is that whatever condition your heart may presently be in, God promises that He "will give you a new heart and put a new spirit within you; I will take the heart of stone out of your flesh and give you a heart of flesh" (Ezek. 36:26). God will literally give you a spiritual heart transplant if you ask Him to do so. Having a new heart within you will be the beginning of your not merely acting like a Christian but truly being one.

A strong, blockage-free heart is essential if we seek to fulfill the first aspect of the Great Commandment. But we can only have a healthy spiritual heart if we make a commitment to constantly guard and strengthen this spiritual core muscle. Recognizing and removing blockages from our heart can sometimes be difficult and painful, but it is something we must do if we truly desire to experience the abundant life that Jesus came to Earth to give us. It is only when we have a heart that is strong, unobstructed and passion-filled that we will be able to love the Lord our God with all our heart, regardless of the challenges, adversity and circumstances we encounter.

WITH ALL YOUR SOUL

When I was in my late 20s, I was the head of a community-based youth center and on the way to leading a major Christian youth movement in Sydney, Australia. I was passionately serving God and so busy that my weeks literally felt like one long day with a series of naps (and these were rare). It was a very exciting time for me. God had given me gifts of leadership and speaking, and many doors of opportunity were opening. I felt like I was living the dream, yet when I would get home and lay my head on my pillow at night—well, actually, in the early hours of the morning—I felt like I was dying inside. When everything was quiet and it was just God and me, the success from the day would fade away and all that would be left was what felt like a gaping chasm in my heart. I was not a happy girl.

No matter how much I accomplished or achieved, I just couldn't seem to find contentment and joy. I didn't know what the problem was. I loved God and everything I was doing, but instead of feeling fulfilled with my destiny, I felt like I was on a treadmill, endlessly running. I wondered when I was going to start feeling complete inside. So in order to fill this void, I just kept working harder and harder, keeping longer and longer hours, hoping sooner or later that my heart would feel fulfilled. This worked for a season because I was entirely focused on all that I was doing and, to be honest, quite amazed at the quantity of work I was able to get done. But eventually, the stress and intensity of my schedule took its toll on my body and I collapsed. Quite literally, in fact. I threw my back out, and my life came to a screeching halt.

For the next three weeks (which felt like an eternity!), my days were spent lying on the couch, keeping very still to avoid the pain of movement. I was forced to stop doing and simply be still.

I was like a fish out of water with this newfound stillness. I felt as though the very breath of my Christianity had been sucked out of my lungs. I had no choice but to literally stop all my Christian activity and *be*. Stripped of my ability to act, I lay there feeling like I had nothing left to offer God. I felt as if I was failing Him because I could not physically do anything for Him. How could I please God when I couldn't even get off my couch?

For the first time in my life, I stopped drowning out the voice of my heart with the sound of relentless activity. As I lay there, feeling like a completely useless Christian, I decided to pick up my Bible. As I flipped through the pages, I came across a verse in Psalms that I had probably read over a hundred times, but that day these words came alive in a new way and arrested my heart: "He brought me out into a spacious place; he rescued me because he delighted in me" (Ps. 18:19, *NIV*).

I just could not get my eyes off those last four words: "He delighted in me." It was like God had a megaphone and was screaming to get my attention: "Christine, I delight in *you*. Not just the thousands of young people you minister to, not just in all that you accomplish in My name, but in you, my own precious daughter." God delighted in me—in *me* with all my faults, me with all my failings, me with my broken past . . . me immobile on a couch! I had been completely undone.

I was totally unprepared for the emotions I experienced that day, and I couldn't stop the flood of tears! It almost felt as if I was having an out-of-body experience. Three boxes of Kleenex later, I looked toward heaven and said, "God, what was *that* all about?" I then heard a voice whisper in my heart, "Read 3 John 2." As I turned to the text, I had no idea that my life was about to be changed forever: "Beloved, I pray that you may prosper in all things and be in health, even as your soul prospers."

That same voice whispered again, "Chris, your soul is not prospering." I was dumbstruck. "God, what do You mean my soul isn't prospering? Look at everything that I'm doing and achieving for You! How could I not be prospering? The ministry is growing, my calendar is full, and we are having great success. I don't understand how I could prosper any *more* for You."

God's response was shockingly clear: "Yes, Chris, I'm aware of everything that you are doing, and so is your body—which is why you're lying there on the couch. I never wanted you to end up in this state. In fact, I tried to get your attention numerous times to warn you about the path you were on, but you were too busy to listen. However, now that you are here, I want to show you some things about your life. Get ready to hear some things you won't want to hear. But if you listen to Me, you will get back on track, run your race and finish your course. Your current condition is actually a reflection of the state of your soul. You have had a battle raging in your soul for years, and it's time to deal with it."

I had been expecting sympathy from God, but instead He was convicting me (albeit very lovingly) that there was a problem in my soul—apparently one that had been there for a long time. Until that point, I had never really thought much about my soul. I knew that my soul was the seat of my emotions and will and, quite honestly, I didn't think there was anything wrong with mine. Obviously God thought differently, and considering He was the creator of the universe and all, it was highly unlikely He was the one who was wrong. Looking back, I can see that my soul was in significantly worse shape than my back, even though I didn't realize it at the time. God is so faithful to reveal to us only the truths we can handle at any given time in our life.

Since I had nowhere to go, I spent a lot of time on that couch reading the Bible and praying. I earnestly sought to understand what God was trying to tell me, reading every Scripture that talked about the soul. But the Holy Spirit kept leading me back to Psalm 23:1-3: "The Lord is my shepherd; I shall not want. He makes me to lie down in green pastures; He leads me beside the still waters. He restores my soul; He leads me in the paths of righteousness for His name's sake."

Well, I was certainly gaining a whole new understanding of the "lying down" concept, as I was horizontal more hours consecutively during this time than I had been over the last several months combined. But as for the "shall not want" part, I was having a hard time relating, as all I wanted to do was go out with my friends to the mall or to a Starbucks—anything that would have gotten me out of the house. Now, as for the "being still" part . . . well, what choice did I have?

As I lay there day in and day out, I eventually did receive a revelation about my soul. I began to realize that if God wanted to restore my soul, then it must have somehow been distorted. I knew that only things that have been damaged, faded or defiled needed to be restored. And then the lights went on.

Leave the Baggage Behind

My life before I became a Christian made me a perfect candidate for the *Jerry Springer* show. I was adopted at birth and was abused in my past, which, needless to say, left me experiencing major rejection, betrayal, shame, guilt and fear (I share this part of my life in great detail in my book *A Life Unleashed*).

Obviously, I had accumulated some baggage over the years, but when I became a Christian, I had no idea that I needed to deal with it. I embraced my new life with passion and enthusiasm, choosing to forget those things that were behind me, and pressing forward to those things that were ahead (see Phil. 3:13). I was not trying to deny my past, rather I sincerely believed that because I was in Christ, I was a *new* creation—the old had *gone* and the new had come (see 2 Cor. 5:17).

I took that to mean that because I was a brand-new creation, my past no longer existed. What I did not realize was that this Scripture spoke of my new *spiritual* condition, not about the condition of my *soul*. The damage and weaknesses that were in my soul realm before I became a Christian lingered after I made the decision to get my life right with God. I still had the same old marred soul. If I had only understood this difference earlier, I would not have ended up on the couch.

Think about it this way: If our physical body has cellulite on it before we become Christians, then even after we've prayed the sinner's prayer, we will still have that cellulite (and we will continue to have it until we stop eating those donuts!). In the same way, if our soul is damaged or wounded before we become a Christian, it isn't miraculously "zapped"—we aren't instantly made whole.

No, being made whole is a process, and if we try to bypass this process, we will remain weak at the core. As a result, eventually all areas of our life will begin to deteriorate—just like my back! Since I was ignorant of my need to be made whole, I jumped into my new spiritual life full steam ahead, still carrying all of that excess baggage.

Right after becoming a Christian, I volunteered for the youth ministry, the new Christian team, the community services team, the small-group leadership team—and every other special project at my church. Before I knew it, I had filled every waking moment with activity. My gifts and talents were quickly recognized, which lead to me being given greater levels of responsibility in a relatively short period of time. Initially, pure zeal and sheer momentum carried me, but it didn't take long before my weak soul muscle began to give way under the weight of my baggage.

I found that although I was working hard and experiencing growth on all fronts, the fruit that I was producing did not line up with the fruit of the Holy Spirit. I did not have a life that was full of "love, joy, peace, longsuffering, kindness, goodness, faithfulness, gentleness, self-control" (Gal. 5:22-23). In fact, my life was quite the contrary.

Many of my BC (before Christian) patterns of behavior soon reemerged because I had never dealt with the issues that were at the root of my behaviors. I thought that I had buried the betrayal, pain, rejection, fear, shame and guilt back there when I had put off the "old self," but the damage my soul had suffered remained. The walls I had built around my life to protect myself were a clear indication of my unresolved issues. I would not allow people to know me too intimately so that I could ensure I would never be hurt again. I was so fearful of not being in control of my circumstances that I demanded control of everything and everyone in my life. Determined to never be rejected again, I was a perfectionist and had no tolerance for mistakes or failure. I was often impatient and harsh and thought that if I could just keep succeeding, everyone would need me and want me. With all of this turmoil in my soul, it is no wonder my life began to unravel.

My responses were not uncommon for someone with my background, but they threatened to keep me subject to bondage—and God wanted me to find freedom. Now that I knew the truth, it was time to be set free. God showed me that although I was born again and Spirit filled, my soul muscle was so emaciated, weak and small that there was little room for the Holy Spirit and His fruit to flow. I had to not only allow God to heal my wounds and strengthen my weaknesses but also to make the choice to develop maturity in order to walk in freedom. Basically, my soul needed a complete overhaul.

It's All About the Fruit

During my time on the couch, I learned that no amount of Christian *activity* compensates for the failure to *be* an authentic Christian. I also came to understand that our authenticity (or lack thereof) is made evident by the fruit that our life is bearing. Jesus said, "By their fruits you will know them" (Matt. 7:20). In other words, if we're to be recognized as Christ's followers, we need to be producing the fruit of His Holy Spirit.

Forced to examine the fruit of my own life, I realized that I lacked any real deep joy and was only happy when things were going my way. Instead of having any real peace, I was constantly striving for perfection and approval. I only had one speed, and that was supercharged. I don't think I even knew how to spell the word "patience." I wanted everything yesterday.

It was sobering to realize that the fruit of the Spirit did not include how well I could preach or how effective I was at giving altar calls. There was nowhere in the Bible where I could find a Scripture that said, "By their *gifts* you will know them" (trust me, I searched the whole Bible). I realized that there could be no doubt that I had been examined by the Lord and found lacking. Deep within me, I came to accept the fact that I had a long way to go in my spiritual walk.

Going to church or praying a prayer doesn't automatically result in the fruits of the Spirit being produced in our life. Rather, the condition of our soul strongly influences the fruit that comes out of our life. The Bible teaches, "Even so, every good tree bears good fruit, but a bad tree bears bad fruit. A good tree cannot bear bad fruit, nor can a bad tree bear good fruit"

(Matt. 7:17-18). Quite simply, if there are areas of our soul that have been damaged in some way, we will inevitably produce bad fruit in those areas. And keep in mind that bad fruit doesn't necessarily point to a horrific past or abuse—it can simply mean that there are areas of the soul that are still not Christlike (and we all have these).

How can we tell what those areas are? By examining our response to the people and events in our life. For example, when we hear that our coworker has received another promotion, do we have the fruit of kindness and rejoice with him, or do we talk about why someone else could do a better job? When we see a grim report on the news, do we freak out, sell our stock portfolio to buy gold and fill our cellars with a six-month supply of imperishable food? Or do we respond with a strong peace in our heart, knowing that God will take care of us? When our best friend has a baby and is back in her pre-pregnancy jeans in fewer than three weeks, can we love and compliment her, or do we try to force feed her pasta alfredo with sausage and buttery garlic bread? And when we finally do get motivated enough to try to shed our post-baby paunch, are we longsuffering with our diets or do we find ourselves rummaging through our couch looking for lost coins at the sound of the neighborhood ice cream truck? As I said, we *all* have areas relating to our soul muscle that need to be strengthened!

If we want to bear good fruit, working on our soul muscle is imperative, regardless of whether or not our past looks like a train wreck (like mine). The goal for all of us is developing the kind of prosperous soul from which flows the qualities listed in Galatians. These fruits cannot be manufactured or externally generated; they result only from soul transformation and an authentic relationship with Jesus.

I realize that this is not rocket science, but so often we tend to overlook the simple truths of life and forget that the profound is usually revealed in the simple. What Jesus is teaching us with the tree metaphor is this: We can *act* out what we are not (at least for a little while), but this will not produce long-term fruit in our life. In other words, an apple can only reproduce apples, because that's what it is at its core. Similarly, if a person has an issue with anger, then no matter how kind and demure she tries to act, eventually a challenging situation will arise and "there she blows"! As long as that anger goes unchecked and unhealed in her soul, she will continue to produce the fruit of anger. The same holds true for fear, jealousy, depression, low self-esteem, and so much more.

Many of us Christians miss out on the abundant life that Jesus has for us because, like this "angry woman in kindness clothing," we haven't taken an honest look at our spiritual core and recognized that our soul needs some work.

Oftentimes, instead of craving the *fruits* of the spirit, which take time to nurture and mature, our efforts are focused on seeking the *gifts* of the Spirit. That's exactly what landed me on my back for weeks! I had obvious gifts in my life—and I put them to good use in a growing church. I took all too seriously 1 Corinthians 12:31, which tells us to "eagerly desire the greater gifts" (*NIV*). Now that's not necessarily a bad thing, as the gifts of the Spirit are given by God to strengthen the Church, but when we seek them at the expense of the deep and often unseen internal work of God, that's when it becomes a problem. In my case, although externally I was moving in the gifts of the Holy Spirit, my soul couldn't sustain me. The fruits of the Spirit were absent in my life, and as a result, my world fell apart.

Sadly, all too often I hear of destinies that have been sabotaged because Christians have been focused on developing the gifts of the Holy Spirit in their life rather than seeking the fruit. They have mistaken a gift given to them by God, which they have done absolutely nothing to merit, as evidence of spiritual maturity. They have convinced themselves that the manifestation of the gift is an accurate measure of their success as a Christian. They could not have been more wrong. When the gifts of the Spirit *on* a person's life are greater than the fruit of the Spirit *in* a person's life, that life will begin to crumble. The indicators of the unbalanced life may be health issues (think of me immobilized on that couch!), broken relationships or an inability to have close relationships, depression, addictions, eating disorders, promiscuity, insecurity, and so much more. This kind of fruit is the outcome of a weak soul muscle.

But here's the great news: We can *choose* to experience the miracle of change! We can change our spiritual core by strengthening and healing our soul muscle. We have God's power working within us to bring about our transformation into the image of Christ that each one of us—and, more important, God—desires. No matter where we've come from or what negative habits we have created in our life, we have a promise from God that we can be someone new. From that soft, responsive heart He has placed within us and His Spirit living on the inside of us, we can learn to live a life that is controlled by the Holy Spirit and not by our flesh.

Regardless of how strong and whole we think we are, we must remember we're all on the journey to Christlikeness and Christian maturity. This maturity is reflected in the alignment of our inner and outer worlds. But the road to maturity is always a process.

As we choose to allow God to enlarge, stretch and strengthen our soul muscle, we will be able to fulfill a second facet of the Great Commandment: loving God with *all* our soul. And as our core begins to change, the spiritual fruits will become the marks that define us as followers of Christ. This outflow of love, joy, peace, patience, kindness, goodness, faithfulness, gentleness and self-control won't be temporary or shallow, because true and lasting transformation has taken place. That's the beauty of a soul restored, renewed and ultimately reborn: When our inner and outer worlds flow from the grace of Christ, we won't have to strive to act like a Christian, because we will simply be one.

WITH ALL YOUR MIND

Catherine Bobbie is our firstborn. She's a beautiful, wonderfully charismatic little princess. And when I say "princess," I mean princess! I'm not referring to one of those little girls who like to play dress up and act like a princess. I'm talking about an honest to goodness, tiara-wearing, legitimate princess—or so Catherine is convinced. Of course, Nick and I have encouraged this behavior. We have given her authentic Disney princess costumes, including gloves, crowns, shoes—everything short of the prince (by order of Nick). What we didn't take into account was the fervor and zeal with which she would embrace her faux royalty (the "faux" part is just between you and me, of course, as Catherine will hear none of that).

She wears one of her favorite princess outfits *everywhere* we go. Dressed from head to toe, she visits her subjects at the grocery store, the shopping mall, restaurants and anywhere else we visit. On a recent dinner outing, Catherine noticed one of the seating areas in the restaurant was closed off—and made a beeline for it. When the waitress graciously pointed out to Nick and me that there was no seating in that particular section (as if the large signs and ropes didn't make it clear enough), Catherine looked up and said very sweetly and sincerely, "I'm a princess. Can't I sit anywhere I want to?"

I have to admit that I love this quality about my daughter. She truly believes that she is special. This is a stark contrast to what I believed about myself when I was a child. It took me years (okay, maybe decades) to walk with the confidence and love for myself that Catherine so naturally has. Nick and I are determined to never quash this quality in her that the world outside has such a tendency to temper.

While some might think that allowing Catherine to believe she's a princess will cause her to grow up with an inflated ego, I believe we're simply reinforcing to Catherine the way that God sees her (and you and me, for that matter). I can't imagine a better start in life for Catherine than knowing who she is in Christ. After all, God calls us His sons and daughters—and that makes us royalty! We are a "chosen people, a royal priesthood, a holy nation, a people belonging to God, that you may declare the praises of him who called you out of darkness into his wonderful light" (1 Pet. 2:9, *NIV*). We truly are sons and daughters of a King, the apple of our heavenly Father's eye. As we come to understand this, it becomes easy for us to declare His praises to others.

I wish I had had Catherine's princess outlook when I was growing up—and I'm sure many of you readers do as well. Even if we did have a semblance of this confidence as children, so many of us were not raised in an environment that enabled us to maintain it into adulthood. In fact, most of us were nurtured in environments that reinforced within us wrong thoughts not only about God but also about others and ourselves.

How we think greatly influences our Christian walk, which brings us to the third and final muscle in our spiritual core: the mind. We must never underestimate the importance of our mind, as it is vital in making our internal transformation an external reality. A strong heart and soul muscle reveal our potential, but it is the mind muscle that unleashes it.

Who Do You Think You Are?

The Bible teaches us that as we think in our heart, so we are (see Prov. 23:7). In other words, who we are today is a result of the thoughts that we have been thinking. Similarly, who we will be tomorrow will be the result of the thoughts we think today. And I'm not talking about the thoughts that we *think* we're thinking about ourselves; I'm talking about what we *truly* think about ourselves deep down.

So many of us believe that who we are today is the result of our upbringing, socio-economic background, education, gender or ethnicity. Of course, all of these factors have played a role in forming who we are, but ultimately our true identity is a result of the patterns of thinking that we have developed as a *response* to our background and circumstances. In short, if we want to change our life, we must change the way we think.

The strength of our mind muscle is not determined by our IQ level, how well we did on our college entrance exams, or how many academic degrees we have obtained. Nor does it depend on how much biblical or theological knowledge we have.

The quality of our mind muscle depends on how much of God's truth (as found in His Word) we believe and apply to our everyday lives.

Again, just as our motivation for working on our heart and soul muscle is to become more Christlike, the goal of a strong mind muscle is to enable us to think more like Jesus. "Let this mind be in you which was also in Christ Jesus" (Phil. 2:5). In order to develop the mind of Christ, we must commit to constantly exercising and readjusting our mind muscle. We all have a ways to go when it comes to thinking like Jesus in every circumstance. In fact, the Bible shows us that there is a huge gap between the way we tend to think and the way God thinks. Isaiah 55:8-9 makes this pretty clear: "'For My thoughts are not your thoughts, nor are your ways My ways,' says the LORD. 'For as the heavens are higher than the earth, so are My ways higher than your ways, and My thoughts than your thoughts.'" This gap between our thoughts and God's thoughts causes many of us to live far beneath our potential in Christ.

So, how do we close this gap? Our thoughts—which for many of us have been shaped by the forces of culture, tradition, our religious experience, the media and our family and friends—have to be supplanted by the truth of the Word of God. Take it from me, in theory this sounds quite straightforward, but in practice, aligning our thinking with God's takes tenacity, determination and personal responsibility (but I know you've got it in you!).

Changing habits of thought that we've had for 10, 20 or 40 years is not easy or instant. Let's face it, we didn't start thinking this way overnight, and we're not going to change overnight. This can be hard to swallow for some, particularly when microwaves spit out a meal in 90 seconds, even the obscurest information appears in .23 seconds thanks to Google, and the unsightly dimples on our thighs can be sucked out in a matter of minutes. At the risk of sounding like a broken record, let me say again: Becoming Christlike is not instantaneous—so be patient.

There is only one sure-fire way to strengthen our mind muscle, and that is by committing ourselves to the process of renewing our mind. Romans 12:2 puts it this way: "And do not be conformed to this world, but be transformed by the renewing of your mind, that you may prove what is that good and acceptable and perfect will of God." I tell you this as someone who has had to walk through this process (and has had to often walk through it again when wrong thinking rears its ugly head). Unsurprisingly, my Jerry Springer-esque past cemented in me some very skewed thinking, which meant that the renewing of my mind was an incredible breakthrough for me. It helped me to move from the prison of my past into the future that God had for me. Even though I was on the road to discovering the importance of strengthening my heart and soul muscles, I knew that embracing my new life in Christ actually hinged on the state of my thought life.

Once I realized that my weak mind muscle was holding me back from the purposes of God, I entered mind-muscle boot camp and was determined to graduate with honors. It was time to replace the mind of Christine with the mind of Christ. As I immersed myself in the Scriptures, I came to recognize how great a disparity there was between the two. I finally understood that nothing in my life would change if I did not change how I thought about everything!

Catch the Right Train

You may have heard the phrase "train of thought." It certainly is a very descriptive and accurate metaphor for describing the way our minds work. Our thoughts are just like a train; they always take us somewhere.

For instance, while I was busily typing the manuscript for this book, I noticed Nick walk past my office doorway with a tub of my favorite ice cream. He did not have to issue an invitation to me (no need, as I have an internal ice-cream honing device—it's one of my God-given gifts). Needless to say, I had a thought (okay, many thoughts) about how beautiful that ice cream would be, melting deliciously in my mouth. I also had another thought about how many calories the tub contained. And, of course, all the while I was thinking about how I was going to meet the deadline for my editors. I had three trains of thought that all pulled into the platform of my mind at the same time, and I had a choice about which of these trains I would board.

Well, I must admit that the ice cream train won the race, and before I finished typing the paragraph that I was working on, I found myself at my freezer, shoveling the ice cream down my throat. Then, spoon in one hand and keystroke in the other, I continued to type. Now, perhaps you would have chosen one of the other two trains to board (then there's the other 98 percent of you who right now are thinking about your favorite ice cream flavor!), but the point I want to stress with this illustration is that if we want to change our destination, regardless of what area of life we're talking about, we have to change the thought trains we board.

Often, we don't realize that we have the ability to make a choice about what we think about. But clearly we do, as we are exhorted to set our mind on things above and not on earthly things (see Col. 3:2). The fact that we are told to *set* our mind means that we have the ability to choose the things that our mind should focus on. This doesn't mean that negative thoughts won't enter our minds—if that were the case, there would be no need to consciously choose to set our minds on the thoughts of God. My point here is that our thoughts are ultimately determined by us.

It was during my mind-muscle boot camp that I discovered this fact. Many of the trains of thought I had at that time about God, the people around me, myself and my destiny were completely contrary to what God thinks, because they were built on the facts of my experience rather than on the truth of His Word. (You only had to look at the condition of my life back then to know that this was true.) I knew that I had to make a change: I had to consciously choose what thoughts I would allow to pull into the platform of my mind.

Armed with this knowledge, and with a firm commitment to exercise my mind muscle, I was ready to go to work. Each time a train of thought that was contrary to the Word of God pulled into the platform of my mind, I would choose not to get on board. Instead, I would purposefully board trains of thought that would take me to the right destination. Philippians 4:8 became my compass: "Finally, brethren, whatever things are true, whatever things are noble, whatever things are just, whatever things are pure, whatever things are lovely, whatever things are of good report, if there is any virtue and if there is anything praiseworthy—meditate on these things." I decided that if a thought did not fit one of these criteria, I would choose not to climb aboard. This is why it's so important to read and meditate on the Word of God. If we don't know what thoughts are contrary to His, how will we ever know what trains to avoid?

At first I thought choosing the right train of thought was going to be impossible because I had failed so many times in the past—and old habits are definitely hard to break. But as I continued to renew my mind on a day-to-day basis (and often on a moment-by-moment basis), I began to notice a change. I started to see this mind shift begin to affect my external behavior and responses.

During this long and often arduous process of renewing our minds, it's vital that we fight off the feelings of frustration that will inevitably come our way. If we don't give up, in time we will experience the fruit of this process in our lives. We'll find ourselves responding to the circumstances of life with the strength, faith and confidence of Christ—all because our mindsets are changing and becoming rooted in God's Word. When we learn to have the mind of Jesus, then we will naturally act like Him, too.

The greatest thing about renewing our mind is the fact that transformation is happening on the inside, in our spiritual core, and this change isn't fleeting. There may be realignment and readjustment from time to time, but this new way of thinking is so engrained that it becomes a new way of life. Instead of yelling at our spouse when we're frustrated, we're able to arrest those thoughts and speak the truth in love. Instead of falling into a pit of depression when we make a mistake or when someone forgets to invite us to a party, we find grace within for others. Instead of eating our way into junk-food heaven when we feel lonely, we reach out to God or a friend for comfort.

Get Back on Track

A few years ago, Nick and I walked through an unexpected and very challenging experience. We found out we were pregnant with our second baby, and we were ecstatic. We were having the time of our lives being Mummy and Daddy to Princess Catherine, and all three of us were very excited to meet this new addition to our family. We waited as long as we could control ourselves to tell our friends all over the world, but once we opened the floodgate, the news spread very quickly. It seemed as if neither Nick nor I could go anywhere without being stopped and congratulated. We were so excited that so many people were enthusiastic about our pregnancy.

Then one day, I went with a friend to a routine doctor's appointment. The doctor began to listen for the baby's heartbeat, which I was very excited to hear for the first time. I held my breath and listened intently for the rapid, miraculous sound of the tiny life inside of me. The doctor seemed to be taking a long time to find it, and by the look on his face I knew that something was seriously wrong. After several minutes, he said the words no expectant woman wants to hear: "Christine, I'm so sorry, but I can't find a heartbeat."

I could never have imagined that a routine appointment might turn so dark and that my great expectations would turn into my greatest fear. My automatic response was denial. I urged the doctor to get a new monitor, because clearly the one he was using was broken. Instead, he scheduled an emergency ultrasound that confirmed that the small life inside of me had died.

To say I was utterly shocked is an understatement, and at that instant my mind was bombarded with so many destructive trains of thought. Sitting on the platform of my mind, just waiting to depart with me on them, were thoughts of guilt. I wondered, *Is this my fault? Have I caused this to happen because I didn't slow down my traveling schedule?* Also on the platform were thoughts of fear: *Is this because I'm almost 40? Are all those grim post-35 pregnancy statistics really true?* And thoughts of doubt: *Did I lack the faith that might have prevented this tragedy? How does this fit with my faith in God's providence?*

In addition, the trains of depression, discouragement, failure and isolation were calling for me to board. These would have inevitably taken me to a destination from which it would have been very hard to return. It was in this moment of great grief and pain that the strength of my mind muscle was going to be tested. Would I still believe that God is good, even when my circumstances were not? Would I be able to trust Him, even though I could not understand why this had happened to me? Was I willing to apply the truth of the Word to this situation despite the disappointment?

My emotions were screaming on the inside. Although the sense of loss and overwhelming sadness I felt were very real, I had to choose to set my mind on things above. The only way that I was going to get through this was by choosing to set my mind on God's eternal Word rather than my current circumstance. I clung to Psalm 23:4: "Yea, though I walk through the valley of the shadow of death, I will fear no evil; for You are with me; Your rod and Your staff, they comfort me," and Psalm 46:1: "God is our refuge and strength, a very present help in trouble."

In the days following my loss, I also took care to be constantly in the house of God. At times my mind muscle was not strong enough to carry the weight of my sadness and I needed to be surrounded by people who would help me to stay on track. I had to be in an environment in which positive trains of thought were constantly passing by the platform of my mind. Eventually, I would jump on one.

It was during one of these worship services that we sang the song "Blessed Be Your Name" by Matt Redman. The lines, "Blessed be Your name on the road marked with suffering, though there's pain in the offering, blessed be your name" were just words to me one week earlier, but now they had become my heart's cry. This song articulated everything that I felt, while keeping me on the right track.

I had that song on repeat in my car, my iPod—just about anywhere I could play music. The words were easy to sing when everything was going well in my life; the challenge was to keep blessing the Lord in my darkest hour. By choosing to magnify God in the midst of my difficult circumstances, I was making Him bigger than the pain I felt.

It was during one of these times of worship that I had what can only be described as a supernatural encounter with God in which He healed my heart. I can't explain it in any other way, but in those moments God did what months of counseling could not have accomplished. He took my grief and filled me with a renewed hope for my future. He truly turned my mourning into dancing and my sorrow into joy. I believe this happened because I had made a choice to take on His thoughts and His ways in the midst of my challenges and adversity. It's only during times of trials that the true strength of our mind muscle is revealed. What is in us will always flow out of us during these times.

I wanted to share this deeply personal story with you to encourage you that no matter what circumstances you might be facing right now, it is possible for you to overcome in the midst of them by taking hold of God's thoughts. It may not always be the easiest thing to do, but trust me: if I can do it, you can do it, too. The same Holy Spirit who helped me strengthen my mind muscle is also there for you, no matter who you are or what your past looks like.

When we make the choice to develop the mind of Christ, we will never regret the time and energy it takes to continually exercise this spiritual core muscle. Our lives will be defined by a deep inner peace and an unshakable joy that can only come from God.

As tempting as it may sometimes be to attempt to bypass the process of renewing our mind, I encourage you to keep persevering. As we transform our thinking and align our thoughts with God's Word, we will be able to make the most of the good times, walk through the dark valleys and never lose sight of God.

Core Transformation—It's Just the Beginning

When I started my Christian walk, I was incapable of fulfilling the Great Commandment of loving the Lord my God with all of my heart, soul and mind, because those areas within me were so completely broken. Because everything in our Christian life stems from our love walk with God, it was crucial that I develop the habit of *daily* strengthening my core spiritual muscles.

I wish I could tell you that change happened in my life overnight, but that is simply just not true. When my trainer, Lisa, told me that it was going to take diligence and time to strengthen my core, she was not joking. And when God says that we are being transformed into His image, He does not mean that this process will happen in an instant. Such spiritual transformation will also require time and effort. As I continue to strengthen my spiritual core muscles throughout my life, I will be able to fulfill this commandment in an increasingly greater measure, but I am not finished yet. We are all God's works in progress!

Immediately after giving us the great and foremost commandment, Jesus continued by saying, "the second is like it: You shall love your neighbor as yourself" (Matt. 22:39). From this, we can see that the natural progression from learning to love God with all of our heart, soul and mind is to then extend this love to our neighbor. Strengthening our spiritual core helps us to more fully love not only God but also other people.

Loving God is only the beginning of being an authentic Christian . . .

GO THEREFORE

"Where are all the people?" I asked Nick. The look he gave me as an answer to my question made me laugh, because it was the same expression he frequently gives to Catherine when she asks him an absurd question. And I guess I could understand his surprise at my words—after all, we were standing in a crowd of hundreds of tourists in one of the most majestic European churches ever constructed. But a lack of people wasn't what I meant.

"No, I mean the Church. Where is the Church?" I said. And there again, staring back at me, was Nick with that look.

"Chris, what are you talking about? We're standing right inside of it," he replied.

"No, I mean the people *in* the church." Before he got another word in, I started to explain myself. "What we're standing in right now isn't the church; it's just a building. And I realize that we are in a crowd of hundreds, but where are all of the people who once made this building a church? When did this stop being a place where people gathered to worship God and instead become an empty building that people pay money to visit?"

Nick finally got it, and his expression changed. As he opened his mouth, ready to respond, I beat him to the punch (what can I say, I was on a roll). "I mean, think about it. It must have taken decades to build this structure, let alone create all the amazing murals and carvings. Many of the men who were part of this building project probably didn't even live to see the finished product or attend one of the worship services. And look at all the intricate details of every single square inch of this place, all to give glory to God. Not to mention the cost! It must have taken some passion to make this all come to pass. What would these people think if they could see that their house of God was now nothing more than a tourist attraction? They would be devastated." (Yes, Nick, like you, often wonders if I ever stop to take a breath.)

Nick and I looked around again, suddenly seeing this amazing building with very different eyes. As the builders labored to finish this magnificent house of God, I imagine the thing that kept them going was a vision of the lives that would be transformed as a result of their tireless efforts. They would have thought about the countless souls who would encounter God in that building, the bodies that would be healed, the marriages restored, the life-giving sermons preached, the prayers prayed, the ministries birthed, the friendships formed and the incredible worship to God that would take place.

As the builders faithfully laid each stone, their purpose was never about the bricks and mortar but about the people who would be impacted and changed once the cement had set. It's true that the actual building was fashioned to be grand and breathtaking, but this was because these men wanted to inspire people by using this building as a reflection, a glimpse, of the excellence and majesty of God. The architecture was not the goal in and of itself—it was only a means to an end. The purpose of the ornate building was to attract people to God (not to the building).

Yet today, Nick and I were standing among hundreds of people waiting patiently to take photos of the building—the bricks and mortar. As they clicked away with their cameras, their comments to one another suggested that they thought they were taking pictures of the church. But the reality was that the Church—that is, the people of God—had left this building long ago, and in their place were the empty pews and beautiful artwork. We could no longer see evidence of the power and life of God's Spirit working in His people, just a building that once housed the church.

I share this experience with you because sadly it is one that I have frequently encountered as I minister in many different cities around the world, and it is the exact opposite of what God designed the Church to be. In the second commandment, Jesus said that we are to love our neighbor as we love ourselves. As the Church, we are called to love our neighborhood and the diverse people represented in it. This is difficult to do if the Church has left the building!

The Church Is People

The word "church" comes from the Greek word *ecclesia,* which is defined as "an assembly" or "called out ones." The root meaning of "church" doesn't pertain to a building but rather to a people. That's you and me!

The apostle Paul actually described the Church as the Body of Christ: "He put all things under His feet, and gave Him to be head over all things to the church, which is His body, the fullness of Him who fills all in all" (Eph. 1:22-23). This would suggest life and activity. Yet at this tourist attraction, there was no sign of a living, active Body of Christ.

Yes, there was a sign erected so that all the tourists could read the history of this church. It said that 200 years ago this cathedral had been a church that was full of life, faith and love. She had been the center of community life and everything revolved around her. She was not only a house of worship but also served the city as the major social justice agency, the main relief organization, and the primary center for medical and aged care. This church had been an intricate part of everyday community life and was not limited or contained by the four walls of a cathedral. Quite the opposite, actually, her influence and reach had gone far beyond the confines of the bricks and mortar that constituted her physical structure. The church had really *been* the Church in the community and was not just *doing* church in a building. She had been living from the inside out— not only loving God with all her heart, soul and mind, but also loving her neighbor as herself.

But where had all the people gone? Jesus had promised that the gates of hell would not prevail against His Church (see Matt. 16:18), so what were we to make of what had happened to this church? Why had the building outlasted the church in this community? Why were people no longer worshiping God in this place? How does something that starts out as a dynamic, living organism—part of the Body of Christ—end up as a dead monument, nothing more than a tourist attraction? And if this church was not a living church, who was actually loving the people of this neighborhood?

I have discovered throughout many years of ministry that a church loses its life and effectiveness at the point it stops *being* the church that God created her to be and starts going through the motions of *doing* church. What is true for the individual Christian remains true for the corporate Body of Christ. As long as a local church is actively involved in its community and in the lives of people, it remains alive, dynamic, vibrant and healthy. This kind of church—the kind the cathedral once was—is being at its core what God created her to be. *THE MESSAGE* explains it this way: "Let me tell you why you are here. You're here to be salt-seasoning that brings out the God-flavors of this earth. If you lose your saltiness, how will people taste godliness? You've lost your usefulness and will end up in the garbage" (Matt. 5:13).

Jesus clearly states that our role as Christians on the earth is a transformational one. We are called the "salt of the earth" (Matt. 5:13), and salt essentially does three major things: It adds flavor, it preserves and it heals. So our task is to bring flavor, preservation and healing to the world around us. This is why it is imperative that we ourselves be personally transformed from the inside out. If we have not been changed, we cannot bring out the "God-flavors" of this earth.

In the same way that salt was never designed to remain in the shaker, the Church was never created to remain insular. We are called to live from the inside out both personally and corporately. God's love flows from within us out into a hurting world. The Church is to be a caring, gracious and inclusive community. Our mandate is to love others as we love ourselves.

Perhaps it is now becoming increasingly clear why it is necessary for us to strengthen our spiritual core and live our Christian lives authentically from the inside out. This is the only way that we can keep our "saltiness" and remain effective Christ-followers. Jesus is clear about our purpose on the earth (to be salt seasoning), and even clearer about where we will end up if we deviate from this purpose (the garbage can).

I'm happy to say that there are many wonderful churches that understand the tenet of Matthew 5:13 and live it out in their communities. These are churches that are actively involved in preaching the good news, in responding to human needs through loving service, in seeking to respond to and transform areas of injustice, and in teaching, baptizing and nurturing new believers. They have a revelation of why the Church is here and they understand that the Church, as God's hands and feet on the earth, is called to operate in the realm for which she was created, namely, a lost and broken world.

We move from *being* the Church to *doing* church when we stop salting and seasoning the world. The fruit of what is happening within the four walls of the church can be measured by the impact of the church outside its four walls. If the activity in our churches does not mobilize people to respond as the Church in the world, we risk becoming introspective and self-serving. In time, this leads to the practice of lifeless religion, empty ritual and irrelevant tradition, which inevitably results in empty buildings. Jesus did not say that He would build an institution or organization. No, He said that He would build

His Church, the Body of Christ, a living, breathing organism made up of people who have been transformed and, in turn, are transforming their world.

The Church is the vehicle that God has created to fulfill His mission on the earth. The people who are the object of this mission normally can be found outside the four walls of the church building. For this reason, every aspect of our church experience should actually empower us to "go into all the world and preach the gospel to every creature" (Mark 16:15). We cannot afford to simply do church on Sunday—we must be the church seven days a week.

Spiritual GPS

Nick and I have a Global Positioning System (GPS) in our car, and Nick loves it. He gets in the car, types in our destination, and immediately the familiar, soothing voice (in my opinion kind of creepy, but comforting) tells us she is coming up with the most direct route for our trip. Nick waits until she is done and then follows her instructions obediently. She has become such a constant companion during our driving outings that we have even given her a name: Matilda. Whenever we find ourselves lost, Matilda can always show us how to get where we want to go. Nick has a special affection for Matilda. He not only loves that he never has to stop and ask for directions, but I think he's also happy because he doesn't have to listen to me telling him my opinions on the best route (which are invariably correct, of course).

I, on the other hand, often get quite annoyed by Matilda. She can be such a know-it-all sometimes, and there are days (although never when Nick is in the car) when I can detect a bit of condescension in her happy, velvety voice. Sometimes just to show her who's boss, I disobey her vocal navigations and pass up the turn she is insisting I make. I think it's funny to hear her start to flip out as I pass up the turn, and then just as I do, go silent. But after a few seconds, the ever-faithful Matilda gets over her meltdown and says, "Rerouting. Please stand by. Rerouting."

When I hear Matilda repeat the phrase "rerouting," it reminds me of the Church's core mission. In a sense, we are God's spiritual GPS, individually sprinkled all throughout the planet (remember the salt). He has placed us in our environments to help people who are lost reroute their lives. Jesus came to seek and save that which was lost (see Mark 16:15), and we as His Body are to continue this mission.

Just like Matilda—only hopefully in a much less annoying voice—we get to influence the people around us who have not yet chosen to believe in Jesus. By the example of our lives and through the relationships we build with people, we can communicate the deep love God has for them and gently steer them closer to His destination for their lives.

I Once Was Lost

I once saw an illustration in a church service that profoundly impacted me. The speaker held up a brand-new, crisp $100 bill and asked the congregation if anyone wanted it. Of course, we all shouted that we wanted it. The speaker then scrunched the note up and jumped on it. He held it up again, only this time all scrunched up, and asked who still wanted it. Again, everyone shouted that we still wanted it. He then described the history of that bill. He proceeded to tell us that the $100 bill had been used to buy drugs, to pay for sex with a prostitute, and then had been stolen. He finished by asking us who still wanted it. Undaunted, the entire congregation immediately raised their hands; we were all still willing to take it. We all understood that the value of money was not determined by what it had experienced or even how it looked. Its value was determined by the Treasury Department that had printed that bill.

The speaker then drew the parallel between our view of the $100 bill and God's view of a lost person. That day, I truly began to understand that the value of humanity, in God's eyes, is not determined by our past, our achievements, our failures or our circumstances. Rather, our value is determined by the love that God has for us. That value is expressed in the fact that Jesus died on a cross for every single one of us, in spite of our short-comings. Jesus did not wait for us to get cleaned up before rescuing us, for "while we were still sinners, Christ died for us" (Rom. 5:8). Even on our worst day, we are worth the blood of Jesus—and nothing is more valuable than that.

We live in a world that often gives more value to animals, the environment and individual rights than it does to people, but there is nothing more costly to God than people. He loves all of us. Further, God places the highest value on lost people. If He didn't, He would never have sent Jesus to seek and save all of humanity. Where would you and I be today if God did not value lost people? All of us were once lost and needed to be spiritually rerouted. And we would still be lost today if believers we know had not taken seriously their role as God's spiritual GPS in our lives.

As I was reflecting on the value of the lost, I recalled an experience that Nick, our daughter Catherine and I once had in a London bookstore. I had decided to look for a shirt in the shop next door, so I left Nick to watch over Catherine for the few minutes I was gone. When I came back, I saw Nick flipping through a motorbike magazine—and there was no sign of Catherine. You know that feeling you get when your heart seems to fall into your stomach? Well, mine felt like it fell to China as the realization hit that we were in a huge foreign city and I didn't know where my daughter was.

Adrenaline pumping, heart racing, I yelled, "Nick! Where is Catherine?!" He quickly looked up. "She is right here," he said. But she wasn't.

I ran out of the shop to search up and down Oxford Street. As I frantically called her name, so many thoughts filled my head: *Had someone snatched her? Had she walked out looking for me? Why hadn't Nick been paying attention?* (Needless to say, this was not my "walking in the peace of God" shining moment.) I was panicked and must have looked like an insane woman as I stopped people in the street, asking, "Have you seen a little three-year-old girl?" I quickly explained to as many people as possible what she was wearing, every detail of her looks, how she walked and talked— I was desperate to find her. I stood on a bench to see over the crowd, all the while yelling her name. The last thing on my mind was how I must have looked, because I did not care what any of these people thought of me. I just wanted my daughter back, and I would do anything to find her.

I went back into the bookstore in a kind of daze, not knowing what else to do in a foreign city (and did I mention that it was rush hour?). The emotions of fear and regret where thick around me, but I knew that I could not allow my mind to go there. I needed to come up with some kind of a plan to find my little girl. I looked around to see if there was anyone else I could find to assist me, and it was then that I saw Catherine sitting quietly behind a bookshelf, looking at one of the dozens of children's books she had pulled off the shelf. I almost flew across the aisle as I grabbed her and squeezed her tight, not knowing whether I should cry, laugh or scream.

After I had overcome the emotion of the moment, I asked Catherine what had happened. Apparently, she had spotted the children's section of the bookstore at the same moment that Nick had turned to pick up the magazine, and had headed over to that section without telling him where she was going. In just a single moment, she and Nick had been separated. Catherine had not even known that she was lost (unlike me, Nick and the several dozens of Londoners I had grabbed on the street). She had not tried to get lost, nor had she found it difficult to end up lost—it had just innocently happened. In fact, the entire time she had been lost, she was having fun, preoccupied with her books. Nevertheless, she had been lost. Nick and I had no doubt about that.

I valued Catherine as my precious daughter (and still do), and I was willing to do anything to find her. I could not bear the thought that she was lost, and I did not want to think about what she could have been going through while she was lost. I am so grateful that this situation was quickly resolved and that Catherine was fine, but it taught me a great lesson: We will do *anything* to seek and save the people that we value. We don't care what we look like or what people are thinking. We throw protocol out the window and do whatever it takes to find those we love.

If we are to seek and save the lost in our world, we must have the same fervent passion and desire that I had in London. Every person is a precious son or daughter of God, and Jesus has sent you and me to go out to find the lost as if they were our own sons and daughters. Sadly, some in the Church have grown complacent in this area, valuing their comfort, routines and traditions over seeking and saving the lost. In effect, they have neglected the Church's core mission.

We don't have to look very hard to discover how much emphasis Jesus put on finding the lost. In fact, the very last words Jesus spoke to His disciples related to exactly this: "He said to them, 'Go into all the world and preach the gospel to every creature'" (Mark 16:15). If we are to become Christlike, then we, too, will seek the lost.

We also see Jesus' passion for the lost in Luke 15, where He speaks about the lost in three consecutive parables (the parables of the lost sheep, the lost coin and the prodigal son). Jesus was clearly passionate about the topic, because nowhere else in Scripture does He do this. Through these parables, Jesus reveals to us the principle that when we have lost something of great value, we'll stop at nothing to find it.

In the first parable of the lost sheep, Jesus says, "What man of you, having a hundred sheep, if he loses one of them, does not leave the ninety-nine in the wilderness, and go after the one which is lost until he finds it?" (v. 4). When the shepherd loses one sheep, Jesus tells us He will leave the 99 that are safe in the fold to search for the one that is lost. This man lives from the inside out—he leaves the 99 on the inside because he realizes the one that is outside the safety of the herd is in danger of being harmed. He also knows that the sheep did not get lost on purpose; it had probably found a ridge with some super tasty grass (just like my daughter Catherine with her dozens of books)! Similarly, people do not get lost on purpose; often they simply get caught up in the turmoil of day-to-day life—just trying to survive, pay the bills, raise their kids. We need to be like the shepherd, willing to do whatever it takes to find the one sheep.

In the second parable of the lost coin, Jesus says, "What woman, having ten silver coins, if she loses one coin, does not light a lamp, sweep the house, and search carefully until she finds it?" (v. 8). The coin did not get lost on its own; it was lost through the carelessness of someone else. Some people are lost through no fault of their own. They have experienced pain and rejection at the hands of others and have been hurt, abandoned, used and abused. Now, they are lost and alone, but like the woman looking for the lost coin, we as the Church must be prepared to light the lamp and leave no corner uncovered until we recover that which is lost.

In the third parable of the prodigal son, Jesus says, "It was right that we should make merry and be glad, for your brother was dead and is alive again, and was lost and is found" (v. 32). The prodigal son was a young man who, because of his own immaturity and selfishness, made a wrong choice and then realized the error of his ways. Despite the fact that he had brought great pain to his father and his loved ones, the father was willing to welcome him back. The father did not condemn, reject or ignore him; on the contrary, at the first sight of his son, he ran to embrace him with open arms! When a lost person comes home to be reconciled with Jesus, we the Church must always have a Welcome Home sign ready, the doors wide open, and the table prepared with the finest feast.

When we seek out that which is lost, we are loving our neighbor as we love ourselves and valuing people as God values them. If we as the Church keep this as our core focus and mission, we will never become an empty building or mere tourist attraction. We will be so occupied and fulfilled with doing what the Church was placed on this earth to do—taking what is inside the Church out into a broken world—that our doors will never close. The lost will be drawn to us because of our open arms and our loving, safe environment. The Spirit of God will be at work in each of us and will flow out into our neighborhoods and communities, making a true and lasting impact on all those we encounter.

INTO ALL THE WORLD

"Nick, wait! Before you come home, can you stop by the store and pick up some flashlight batteries?"

Luckily, Nick heard me before he hung up. "Are you kidding?" he replied. "I just bought a huge new pack last week."

"Catherine." That was all I needed to say to him.

Nick laughed and said, "Your daughter is obsessed with that thing!"

"Hey, why is she *my* daughter when you're referring to quirky things but she's *your* daughter when she's doing something clever or cute?"

"I was simply comparing her to your love to be a light in the darkness," he replied. (One thing I love about my husband is that he is *very* quick on his feet.)

"Nice comeback," I said, impressed. We both laughed as we hung up the phone.

He was right about Catherine; she is obsessed with flashlights. She is constantly taking our emergency flashlights from the drawer and carrying them around with her. When she first discovered them, she would walk around all day with a flashlight by her side, shining it everywhere. The only problem was that during the day, it really didn't have much of an effect. I would try to explain to her that flashlights are really not of great use during the day. After all, how much can you illuminate a room that is already well lit? But you know how kids are—most of their fun is had in discovering new things. So off Catherine would go with her flashlight, endlessly shining it all day long until the batteries wore down (which happened quite frequently).

I'll never forget the first time Catie actually "got it" when it came to how a flashlight was really supposed to be used. Nick and I were in her room putting her to bed, and we turned off all the lights so that it was pitch black. It was priceless to see the look on her face when Nick turned the flashlight on and she realized how bright the beam was in a dark room. We all laughed as we chased the beam around the room and made funny hand-shadow puppets on the walls.

We thought that this realization would alleviate Catherine's need to tote the light around with her throughout the day and make "flashlight fun" an evening game (thus saving a bundle on batteries). However, it had the opposite effect! We had unwittingly made it even more of an adventure for her. Now, every day was a challenge for her to find the darkest places she could so that she could light a path for all her toys to find their way. For the next two weeks, my afternoons were spent in the dark as Catherine took my hand and guided me through the maze of furniture. She'd turn off the lights and say, "Mummy, take my hand. I'll help you find your way." And this one was the cutest: "Mummy, watch your toes! Let me shine the light on the chairs so you won't bang your foots." Moments like these make concerns about wasted batteries go out the window!

I love how passionate Catherine was as she led me carefully around the furniture. Just the thought of me hurting myself in the dark deeply concerned her, as was evidenced by her shining the flashlight meticulously in every possible corner so that I didn't bump my "foots." She is so proud of herself, because with her little light, she is able to bring me to a place of safety.

As I was sharing this game of ours with a close friend, I realized that it was a perfect illustration of how we as Christians are to be in this world. Just as Catherine is so excited to shine her light for me, we are called to shine our spiritual light for others.

Jesus said, "I am the light of the world. He who follows Me shall not walk in darkness, but have the light of life" (John 8:12). Those of us who are followers of Jesus have the privilege to walk in His light and to experience the life that is illuminated by His Word. But this light within us is not just for ourselves—it is meant to be shared with the whole world. Jesus tells us:

> You are the light of the world. A city that is set on a hill cannot be hidden. Nor do they light a lamp and put it under a basket, but on a lampstand, and it gives light to all who are in the house. Let your light so shine before men, that they may see your good works and glorify your Father in heaven (Matt. 5:14-16).

We have a responsibility to shine Christ's light wherever we are. As with salt, light is an agent of transformation. Light and darkness cannot coexist. Whenever light encounters darkness,

darkness is dispelled. In a world full of darkness, hopelessness, pain and anguish, people are looking for direction, answers to their confusion and some semblance of hope for their future. That's why Jesus tells us to shine our light. The light in our life helps those around us find a way through the darkness and points them toward the life God has waiting for them.

It is as we shine our light in the midst of this darkness that people will be attracted to God, His love, His grace and His mercy. The prophet Isaiah declares, "Arise, shine; for your light has come! And the glory of the LORD is risen upon you. For behold, the darkness shall cover the earth and deep darkness the people; but the LORD will arise over you, and His glory will be seen upon you. The Gentiles shall come to your light, and kings to the brightness of your rising" (Isa. 60:1-3). Isaiah tells us that the light of Christ is attractive, magnetic and transformational. The key is to ensure that we actually let our light shine in our everyday life.

This Little Light of Mine . . .

As sharers of God's light, we choose the intensity of the light that we shine into our world. The strength of our spiritual core actually determines whether we are a faint flickering candle, a 75-watt light bulb or a stadium spotlight. If our core is weak, broken and fragmented, then our light is dimmed, impeding our effectiveness in sharing Christ's light. The degree to which we allow the light of Christ to transform our own lives determines how far our light shines in a dark world.

When I was a university student, my heart, soul and mind muscles were very weak. Although I had recommitted my life to

Christ during this time, I was still full of shame and fear, and I suffered from a deep sense of rejection and low self-esteem. I was surrounded by the normal activities of campus life—not only study groups, all-night cramming for exams and lots of pizza, but also endless parties, drinking, immorality, drugs and the like. Although I did not actively participate in the latter, looking back I can now clearly see that I was not making any positive difference in the lives of my friends who were. There was one afternoon in particular when this was made evident to me, and it changed me forever.

I had my head in a book, studying, when I heard a familiar voice call my name several times. I looked up and saw my friend Sharon running toward me, breathless with excitement. I was actually very relieved to see the face of my friend at that moment. She had been out of touch for three days, which was very unlike her, and I had started to worry about her. As she rushed toward me, I could see that she was very excited about something. The closer she got, the more I realized that, except for her bright smile, she looked awful. It was all very strange, but before I could ask her about her appearance, she blurted out everything she had experienced during the last 72 hours.

"Chris, you're not going to believe where I've been this weekend!" she began. "It was the most awesome experience I have ever had in my whole life! I haven't even been home yet because I wanted to come and find you first thing. I went to this party called a rave. I tried this amazing thing called ecstasy. Chris, I had the most incredible time of my life! Everyone there was taking this new drug, and we experienced three days of nonstop love, peace and joy. I wish you had been there, too.

You would've been in heaven—I know I was. I think I have laughed more in the last few days than I have in my entire life! I didn't want you to miss out on this experience, so I saved some for you. You're not going to believe how wonderful it makes you feel."

She pulled an ecstasy tablet out of her pocket and handed it to me. "You will love it, and you must come with me the next time they have a party like this. There might even be one this weekend. I can't wait for you to experience it!" I was so shocked by everything I had just heard that all I could do was sit there with my mouth open, still holding the small ecstasy tablet she had thrust into my hand.

Before I could hand it back to her and tell her I didn't want it, she had excused herself to go home and take a much-needed shower. Off she went, as excited as she had come—and there I sat just watching her leave. I felt a sense of deep regret come over me and the sting of tears began to fill my eyes.

I had been a Christian the entire time I had known Sharon. The passion that I had just witnessed in those last few moments from her (about a drug) was 10 times more than any I had ever displayed to her about my faith in Jesus. In fact, I had been afraid to talk too much about Christianity with her because I didn't want her to think I was a freak or that I was trying to shove Jesus down her throat. To be honest, from where I was standing, her life seemed so perfectly together. She was popular, smart, rich, had a steady boyfriend, and I couldn't imagine how I would ever convince her that she needed God.

After seeing her level of excitement about something as corrosive as this three-day drug-fest, I realized I had obviously been very mistaken in my assumptions about Sharon's life. Even though she had appeared to have everything on the outside, on the inside she was empty, without purpose and searching for something. But she didn't know what that something was.

Like anyone without Christ, Sharon was lost and on a path that would lead to destruction. I was particularly stunned at the fact that, even though I had been involved in Sharon's life on a daily basis, I had in no way been bringing any light to her darkness. The light of Christ in my life was so dim that it had no transformative influence on her life.

As Sharon recounted her weekend at the rave party to me, it was clear that the things that had most affected her were the feelings of love, joy and peace she experienced. These were obviously missing from her life, or she wouldn't have been so eager to fill that void with ecstasy. The truth is that Sharon should have been able to see love, joy and peace—the fruits of the Holy Spirit—in my life and have wanted to ask me how she, too, could experience that kind of life. Instead, my light was so diffused that Sharon had to seek counterfeit light by taking a drug.

That day, I came to the grim realization that I had missed a God opportunity. He had put me in Sharon's life for a reason— so that I could be the light of Christ that would draw her into relationship with Him. However, instead of being like my daughter Catherine, *more* than eager to lead anyone she could with her flashlight, I had kept the light to myself and was partly responsible for keeping Sharon in darkness.

My spiritual core was weak, and I didn't have the battery power on the inside to bring illumination to those around me. It was at that moment I came to understand that my own fear and brokenness had stopped me from switching on the light where it was most needed.

Before this revelation, I had thought that I was being a strong Christian simply because I didn't do what many of my college friends did, like getting drunk, taking drugs or sleeping around. I was defining my Christianity by what I *was not* doing, completely forgetting about what it was that I *should be* doing. The goal of my university years should have been not only to abstain from "bad" behaviors but also to actually bear witness to the abundant life of God living in me.

Although Sharon was aware that I was a Christian, for all she knew, the only thing that made me different from her was that I didn't do all the typical stuff (drinking and partying) that she did. In essence, I presented to Sharon a version of Christianity that was all about what Christians can't do. This to a girl who liked to party! Sharon didn't see the fruit of an authentic relationship with God at work in me. All she could see was what I wasn't doing rather than the good works I should have been doing.

When Jesus said that people would see our good works and give glory to the Father in heaven, He was not talking about making religious behavior modifications but rather about displaying the fruit of an authentic Christian life. These actions flow from the fruit of the Holy Spirit working in our lives and are characterized by kindness, mercy, justice, love and compassion. God would have been glorified if I had focused on shining my light in this way rather than emphasizing only what I could not do.

In hindsight, I can see why the "University Christine" shone such a tiny little light. It wasn't that I was purposely trying to hide my light under the proverbial basket, but rather because

I was so weak and scarred in my core. I didn't have the courage to share my faith openly and give my friends access to my world.

I'm not suggesting that I should have accompanied Sharon to rave parties, but I should have been willing to engage in her life deeply enough to come to know what she was really feeling and thinking. Instead of being intimidated by the darkness her life represented, I should have been the catalyst for some honest, deep communication. Then perhaps I might have influenced the choices she made. I needed to be *in* her world but not *of* her world so that through me, God could bring lasting change to her world.

In the World But Not of It

If I had been brutally honest with myself, I would have seen that my own fear was the real reason that I did not allow myself to get intimately involved in Sharon's life. I was afraid that if I moved too close to the darkness she represented (the big dark world), I would be swallowed up by it. With my core (heart, soul and mind) as weak as it was, I didn't know if I had the strength to resist the temptation. My light was a dim, barely flickering candle. So what did I do? I stayed as far away from Sharon's dark world as I could but close enough to ensure that I still had someone to sit with at lunchtime.

I know some of you can relate to this (don't pretend you can't!). You became a Christian, and all of a sudden you thought you were no longer allowed to smile! You started toning down your wardrobe in favor of beige, stopped wearing lipstick, and would not leave the house after 9:30 at night to avoid temptation (okay, this may be a little extreme, but you get my point).

When our spiritual core is weak, we find it hard to remain in the world without succumbing to temptation. We don't go to our neighbor's party in case they're serving alcohol. We are afraid that we'll accidentally pick up a drink, and then another, and then all of a sudden we'll be drunk (which is a sin)! In our head, not going makes more sense than taking the time to develop the fruit of the Spirit called self-control. We end up hiding our light away just in case it gets extinguished by a gust of wind called temptation.

But Paul assures us in 1 Corinthians 10:13 that "no temptation has overtaken you except such as is common to man; but God is faithful, who will not allow you to be tempted beyond what you are able, but with the temptation will also make the way of escape, that you may be able to bear it." Now, I'm not saying that we should throw wisdom to the wind. For example, if someone has had a real problem with alcohol in the past, the pub on a Friday night is probably not the best place for that person to shine his light. The point I'm trying to make here is that if we have an unfounded fear of the world that causes us to retreat from the world, we will fail to bring light to the world—and a dark world will remain devoid of the living Church.

When the Church retreats from the world, she becomes a fortress. She is seen as little more than an irrelevant, archaic, outdated, decaying institution on the fringes of society. Sadder still, she becomes filled with people who are of the world but not in it rather than people who are in the world but not of it. Now, this might sound like mere semantics, but there's a big difference!

If we choose to hide away instead of being changed from the inside out, then inevitably we bring all the baggage, attitudes and behaviors of our pre-Christian life into church with us. We may never go to a movie again (unless it's G-rated), get a tattoo, wear an earring or drink alcohol, but if we have never dealt with things like bitterness, unforgiveness, greed, lust, envy, malice and guile, they will still be there under the surface. The fact that they still remain in us is what makes us the same substance as the world. It is when God's Spirit is at work in us and changes our core that we become different from the world. Only then can we be in the world but not of it.

Jesus prayed that we, the Church, would do what He came to Earth to do—to bring His light to people in a tangible way. He said:

> I do not pray that You should take them out of the world, but that You should keep them from the evil one. They are not of the world, just as I am not of the world. Sanctify them by Your truth. Your word is truth. As You sent Me into the world, I also have sent them into the world (John 17:15-18).

I think it's so telling that Jesus specifically said that He did not ask that His followers be taken out of the world. Quite the contrary, He said that He is sending us into the world. In the twenty-first century, this world is filled with immorality, iniquity, crime, violence, greed, chauvinism, gossip, sexism, slander, racism—and the list goes on. Jesus knew that if we were personally transformed by His Spirit and had a strong spiritual core, our light would shine forth brightly from a place of strength and we would simultaneously remain holy in the midst of the darkness.

The world that Jesus has sent us into is not a distant, far-off land in the remote regions of the earth but the place in which each of us conducts our everyday life. This world comprises our homes, neighborhoods (and our neighbors), schools, colleges and workplaces. This world was never supposed to be a threat to the Church but rather the mission field of the Church, which, through Jesus Christ, has the power to change our world rather than be changed by our world! But it will take each and every one of us to personally rise up and take our light to the world. Instead of hiding from the world or being overwhelmed by the evil of it, we need to strengthen our spiritual cores and trust in the power of the Spirit at work in us.

AND PREACH THE GOSPEL

"Christine." Nick was using his pay-attention-to-me voice.

"Yes," I said as I realized my eyes were looking in his general direction but my mind was somewhere else.

"Did you hear anything I just said?"

"Umm," I quickly tried to rewind the sound track inside my head, but I couldn't seem to make any sense of the words.

"Honey, if you would just focus for a minute, you would be so glad you did. I bought you this computer so that you could use it for more than typing. You can research anything you want. You can go onto iTunes and download almost any song you want. You can edit photos, even video! You can keep your entire schedule on it and record voice notes to yourself. And look at all these cool widgets you can download."

When it comes to computers, Nick is the super wiz of the family, with Catherine just a few steps behind (you know it's bad when you're asking your five-year-old to help you log on). Nick is amazing when it comes to technology. With his computer, he can do all kinds of neat things with photos, videos,

PowerPoint, music—you name it. I don't know the computer lingo for all the stuff he does, but he and that computer are really impressive!

He is also a really great teacher when it comes to new technology—I'm just a terrible student. I'm honestly excited to see the computer do everything that Nick says it can do, but when he starts explaining to me how I can do the same, everything starts to go fuzzy. You know the kind of fuzzy you would see on the TV when you were a kid and it was really late at night (before television programming went 24/7)? The screen would go snowy and the sound was just static. That's what my brain does when Nick starts his tech talk.

So here I am, a forward thinker in almost every area, using my state-of-the-art computer as little more than a typewriter. Even though my computer has all of these really colorful icons across the bottom of the screen, I'm afraid to click on any of them. I wonder, *What do I do once the program opens? What if I can't get out of the maze?* So I just look for the big *W* icon that stands for MS Word (it's familiar to me and it's also a comforting blue color), and I do what I have always done—use my laptop as a word processor. Besides, Nick is never too far away if I have something more complicated to do, like sending an e-mail attachment.

Although it can be painful to watch Nick smile and roll his eyes when I ask him to show me for the hundredth time how to navigate the programs, he is always willing to help. But never without the speech. "Chris, if you only knew how many options you have at your fingertips . . . this computer was made to do so much more than what you're using it for. You have practically unlimited memory, and every program you could possibly need has been loaded onto this computer. All you need to do is click on this button . . ." and that's where he loses me. My brain turns to snowy static.

Here we have a girl (that would be me) who has a computer that has the capacity to do all that she needs done, but she does not take the time to learn the programs. She remains ignorant of all that it can do and, worse still, expects everyone else to do the work she could easily do for herself, if only she would take the time to learn how.

You may well laugh at my computer illiteracy, but think about Nick's frustration with me in terms of how God must feel about us at times. He has not only saved us but has also given us His Holy Spirit so that we can achieve His mission on the earth. Yet so many of us are not aware of the reasons why God has given us His Spirit, nor do we do all that we could with the power of the Holy Spirit working in us. Like me with the computer, we often wait for everyone else to do what we could easily do if we would simply apply ourselves.

I'm afraid we can't claim ignorance on this one. Jesus clearly tells us why we have the power of the Holy Spirit working in our lives:

> The Spirit of the LORD is upon Me, because He has anointed Me to preach the gospel to the poor; He has sent Me to heal the brokenhearted, to proclaim liberty to the captives and recovery of sight to the blind, to set at liberty those who are oppressed; to proclaim the acceptable year of the LORD (Luke 4:18).

The Spirit of the Lord is upon us to enable us to reach out beyond ourselves and to help others. God has not empowered us with His Holy Spirit just so that we can have a peaceful Christian lifestyle. He has not given us His Spirit just so that we can go to church, avoid the world, prophesy and pray in tongues. Don't get me wrong, all of that is great, but if we stop there, the Holy Spirit inside of us is a little like my computer in my hands. Just as my computer barely scratches the surface of all it was designed to do, so too the Holy Spirit is unable to unleash His awesome power within us. The Spirit of the Lord is upon us so that we can be like Jesus, bringing hope and life and liberty to a lost, sick and broken-hearted humanity.

Right now you might be thinking, *I have my hands full just getting the kids out the door for school, planning something that resembles a healthy dinner, reading that report before work in the morning and getting the laundry done. When do I have time to preach the gospel to the poor and release the captives? I can't find the car keys, let alone the keys to the prisoners' cell door!* If so, you're not alone. Most of us read Luke 4:18 and experience a bit of brain snow—you know, the kind I suffer from every time Nick talks computer. We simply don't compute how we can play any role in God's grand scheme for the world.

The good news is that we don't have to do this all alone. God has given us the Holy Spirit who enables us, comforts us and empowers us (and gives us a gentle prod whenever necessary!) to help us to fulfill His mandate. Acts 1:8 makes this clear: "You shall receive power when the Holy Spirit has come upon you; and you shall be witnesses to Me in Jerusalem, and in all Judea and Samaria, and to the end of the earth."

Jesus said that the Holy Spirit gives us the power to be His witnesses throughout the earth. I hope you noticed that Jesus did not say He would give us the power to *do* the witnessing but rather to *be* witnesses. This is because the power that we need to effectively witness to others essentially flows from being an authentic witness ourselves. We must *be* before we *do*. I am in no way suggesting that we do not proactively proclaim the gospel to our friends, neighbors and other people with whom we come into contact, but I sincerely believe that we need to not only preach the gospel but also live in the power of the gospel. To be a witness for Christ, we must be bearing witness to the truth of His Word. This generation needs to see that the gospel "works" in our lives before they will believe that it is true.

It is therefore crucial that we continue to strengthen our spiritual core and live an authentic Christian life from the inside out. If I was still broken, wounded and rejected, I would have no power to preach good news to the poor. If I had not found freedom, how could I shine a light for others to find theirs? If I was still brokenhearted because of my past, how could I help to heal someone else's broken heart? And if I was still in captivity, how could I possibly proclaim liberty to others? More than any words, program or doctrine, it's our very life that speaks the loudest. As we live out the gospel in every aspect of our lives, we build a platform from which to proclaim it to others.

Can I Get a Witness?

Being a witness is not a program; it's a lifestyle. God has given us the power to be a witness in our seemingly insignificant day-to-day life. At the school gate, at mothers' group, at the grocery store, at the gas station, at the sports club, at the office, there are endless opportunities to bear witness to His truth. We show our "neighbor" what authentic Christianity looks like in a practical way through the way we live our life. This is often not spectacular, but it is truly supernatural!

When Jesus was speaking to Pilate, He said, "You say rightly that I am a king. For this cause I was born, and for this cause I have come into the world, that I should bear witness to the truth. Everyone who is of the truth hears My voice" (John 18:37). Jesus said that He came to earth to *bear witness* to the truth, and this has profound implications for each and every one of us.

Jesus did not come only to proclaim the truth (which is imperative) but also to ensure that every aspect of His life was bearing witness to that truth. Similarly, our lives ought to be bearing witness to the truth of God's Word. This includes our relationships, our lifestyles, our habits, our spending priorities, the moral choices we make and our values and dreams. We ought to have a standard that is different from that of non-Christians because we are supposed to be bearing witness to His truth. Our lives should be built according to the Word of God. If we fail to live according to the Word we preach, then we will have little or no impact on the world around us.

Which brings us to our need for the power of the Holy Spirit. One reason that we have focused so much on developing and strengthening our spiritual core is because everything that we do flows from this. In order to live in a way that bears witness to the truth, we must be strong on the inside.

This may sound very basic for many of you, but so often we overlook the simple things and miss out on the life of Christian

influence we were meant to live. Not every one of us is called to
stand on a platform and preach (I can almost hear sighs of relief)
or sign up for the church evangelism team, but we are *all* called to
live a life that bears witness to His truth. Acting like a Christian
does not bear witness to the truth, but *being* a Christian does.

I love the way Jesus did not complicate His commission but
made it attainable for us all. He said, "Follow Me, and I will
make you fishers of men" (Matt. 4:18). This means that whatever our personality, gifts and talents, Jesus will take these and
make of us "fishers of men." The word "make" actually means
"to shape, to frame, to form, to construct." In this Scripture,
Jesus is saying that He will take us as we are and literally transform us into fishers of men. This is not a gift or a calling; it is
what each of us is becoming as we continue to follow Christ.
As we are transformed, becoming more Christlike, we will
naturally draw other people to Jesus. Regardless of our past,
disposition or personality type, a true sign that we are followers of Christ is that we are becoming fishers of men.

Can you imagine how quickly we could fulfill Christ's
mission on the earth if each of us took up the challenge to be
a witness to the world? Statistics vary, but let's just assume
that there are two billion Christians on Earth today. If every
one of us took seriously our mandate to transform our communities by being salt and light, we could achieve in one week
what the greatest preaching evangelist could not possibly
achieve in a lifetime. Can you see why we must stop acting like
Christians and start *being* Christians? It will take each and every
one of us to do our individual part in order for the Church as
a whole to fulfill her mandate.

It always challenges me when I read what Jesus told His disciples about the harvest of souls before them: "The harvest truly is great, but the laborers are few; therefore pray [to] the Lord of the harvest to send out laborers into His harvest" (Luke 10:2). Notice that Jesus does not say that the *Christians* are few but rather that the *laborers* are few. We can get the job done if we all choose to participate in Christ's mission instead of just sitting on the sidelines at Christian events. It is a labor to bring in the harvest—one that requires all hands on deck.

It's a common misconception that a laborer in the harvest must be one of the gifted few in the Church who have been given some kind of special holy ordinance from heaven in order to talk to someone about Jesus. Many of us believe there are special units in God's heavenly army that are outfitted from head to toe with all the latest life-saving gadgets so that they—and only they—can swoop in with their stealth helicopters to grab the unsaved from the jaws of spiritual death. Well, sorry to disappoint you, but you are a member of God's special-forces team. You are it! You and I are the people Jesus was talking about when He said, "You are the light" and "You are the salt." He has no Plan B—no designated reinforcements are about to drop out of the sky.

Of course, evangelists have a place in the Body of Christ, but their primary task is to train and equip the Body of Christ to be witnesses. "And He Himself gave some to be apostles, some prophets, some evangelists, and some pastors and teachers, for the equipping of the saints for the work of ministry, for the edifying of the body of Christ" (Eph. 4:11-12). Nevertheless, we are all responsible for both witnessing and proclaiming God's truth to a lost world. Admittedly, some are called to do this to large crowds, but most Christians will work this out among the people in their world.

We must never shy away from the proclamation of the gospel of Jesus Christ, "for it is the power of God to salvation for everyone who believes" (Rom. 1:16). And even though we know that not everyone will respond to the gospel in a positive way, we still are responsible for its proclamation.

Being Involved Is the Key

If we are living an authentic Christian life from the inside out, we can never be ashamed of the gospel. We are living testimonies of its transforming power in our own lives, and we are passionately committed to seeing it work in the lives of others. When we truly love our neighbor as we love ourselves, we cannot help but proclaim this life-saving Word to them. Yet in order to be able to share the gospel with our neighbors, we must be willing to stop and take notice of what is going on in the lives of others.

Jesus always stopped and noticed what was going on around Him. He brought restoration to the physically sick, emotionally damaged and spiritually destitute. Although He was on a mission to save all of humanity, He was never too busy to notice the crippled man by the pool, the woman at the well, or the woman with the hemorrhage. He was always on the way to somewhere else, but He was ever prepared to be interrupted and to get involved in the lives of individual people whose paths He crossed.

In our fast-paced modern world, we can often feel that we can barely keep up with our own lives let alone take on the interruption and inconvenience of someone else's. But if we are to truly *be* a Christian and not just *act* like one, we must be prepared to love our neighbors as we love ourselves and express this through our tangible involvement in their life. In Matthew 25:31-46, Jesus tells us that we must feed the hungry, visit those in prison, clothe the naked and take a stand against injustice, inequality, disease and poverty. He says that "inasmuch as you did it to one of the least of these, My brethren, you did it to Me." It is clear from this passage of Scripture that the "because" of our Christianity is only evidenced by acts of practical service that flow from our love of God and our neighbor.

In a world longing for authentic relationship, we need to get up close and personal with those who are hurting and lost. The Church must be seen, felt and heard in the trenches of human experience. The Bible teaches that from the beginning of time, God has prepared good works for you and me to do. We are saved by grace for good works, "for we are His workmanship, created in Christ Jesus for good works, which God prepared before-hand that we should walk in them" (Eph. 2:10).

I want to reiterate that these good works are not necessarily spectacular. They could include shopping for a friend or neighbor who is incapacitated, visiting the sick, taking time to listen to a coworker's personal struggles, helping someone in need or visiting the aged in a nursing home. Yet each one of these "ordinary" good works contains within it the seed for a supernatural encounter.

It is easy to become overwhelmed with all of the needs in the world—and to think that our small contribution will not make any real difference. The thing that we must understand is that we are only responsible for the good works that God has called *us* to do. We cannot do everything, but we must all do something. We do not need to assume responsibility for anybody else's good works but simply do what we are supposed to do. If we all did this, I believe that we would fulfill Christ's mission on the earth.

We must begin to value our seemingly mundane lives and routines, understanding that each day God has opportunities waiting for us to meet the needs of others. No matter where we live, we are all surrounded by people who need to know the practical love of God. We cannot just sit back and pray and hope that *somebody else* does something. James teaches us:

> What does it profit, my brethren, if someone says he has faith but does not have works? Can faith save him? If a brother or sister is naked and destitute of daily food, and one of you says to them, "Depart in peace, be warmed and filled," but you do not give them the things which are needed for the body, what does it profit? Thus also faith by itself, if it does not have works, is dead (Jas. 2:14-17).

If we are to perpetuate a Christianity that can truly change our world, our faith must be accompanied by good works. When we shine our light on these works of grace, then God Himself is glorified. And as we continue to love the Lord our God with all of our heart, soul and mind, we ensure that our works flow from our love rather than a sense of duty. For if we truly love God, the Creator, then our love cannot help but joyously overflow to His creation—our neighbors.

People Are the Goal

People are not an interruption in our lives; they are why we're here. If we do not stop and get involved in what others around us are doing, someone or something else invariably will—perhaps the neighborhood drug dealer, the New Age spiritualist, the pimp or the partying friend. The Spirit of the Lord God is not upon *these* to set the captives free, but upon us, the Church of Jesus Christ. It is our responsibility to get involved.

Jesus' parable of the Good Samaritan in Luke 10:25-37 emphasizes the importance of getting involved. It begins with a Jewish man who had been robbed and left for dead on the side of the road. Three different people encountered this unfortunate man that day, but only one responded the way Jesus would have us respond. Two of the people, a Pharisee and a Levite, were religious men. By virtue of the fact that they both were Jews, they should have stopped and attended to the man. However, instead of seeing this man as the goal of their religious duty, they saw him as an interruption. They had places to go and people to see, and they did not have the time to stop and assist the wounded man.

The third man, the Samaritan, was the last person who should have stopped to help the beaten man, as the Jews hated the Samaritans, thought they were dogs and treated them accordingly. The Samaritan could have come up with a list of reasons for why he should just let that Jewish man die on the side of the road. But instead, "when he saw him, he had compassion. So he went to him and bandaged his wounds" (Luke 10:33-34).

It's possible that the Pharisee and the Levite felt some sense of pity when they saw the man lying in the ditch. However, whatever it was they felt, it did not compel them to take any action. The Samaritan, though, *did feel* true compassion because he crossed the street and got involved. Real compassion is more than an emotional feeling—it always leads us to action.

Like the others, the Samaritan was also on his way somewhere—yet he stopped and lifted the bloodied man out of the ditch and put him on his donkey. He wasn't worried about the condition of his freshly pressed robe or the danger of contracting a disease. He simply got involved at the man's point of need. Helping this man cost the Samaritan both his time and treasure—he did not just pray for him and then leave him on the side of the road. Rather, he gave the man transportation, lodging and provision. This is why Jesus said that this Samaritan man was the only one that truly loved his neighbor.

If we were to look at this story in the context of our world, there are a lot of people lying in ditches, metaphorically speaking. Outwardly they may not be bloodied and bruised, but inwardly, they're broken, hurting and looking for answers. It is imperative that we as the Church consciously *choose* to get involved in their lives.

I recently had my very own Good Samaritan opportunity. As I sat in my living room, which faces out to the street, I noticed one of my neighbors packing up a truck with various items. I didn't give it much thought, as there were a lot of garage sales at that time of the year and I assumed he was going to drop the things off somewhere. However, the next day, I was talking to this man's wife, Nicole, and after a few minutes of chatting, she broke down and started weeping. She revealed to me that her husband had left her and their two children for another woman.

It was at that point that I realized that what I had witnessed the day before was the farthest thing from a garage sale. I had seen the whole horrible event unfold as I sat comfortably in my office.

At that moment, as I stood in my driveway and watched my neighbor weep, I had a choice to make. Would I simply hug my neighbor, tell her I was sorry and pray for her? Or would I choose to get involved in her pain? In all honesty, the former would have been simpler, as I had just given birth to Sophia and was still recovering.

Instead, I chose to get involved and invited Nicole and her kids to my home for dinner. During the next few weeks, we spent several hours crying, talking, and crying some more. The Spirit of the Lord was on me, because He sent me to reach into Nicole's life to help heal her broken heart. By being involved in her world, I was able to shine the light of Christ in the midst of very dark circumstances, and what could have been simply another statistic turned into a great testimony.

By getting involved in Nicole's world, I built a platform from which I could proclaim the gospel to her. If I had tried to do this without the corresponding good works, I do not think she would have listened. Because she knew that I was genuinely concerned about her plight and that of her two children, she was open to hearing about the life, hope and liberty that could be found in and through a relationship with Jesus Christ. Over time, and through a series of circumstances, I am thrilled to say that Nicole became a follower of Christ. The great news about this is that she and her children are now firmly planted in a local church and are building their lives on the foundation of God's Word. Their mourning has been turning into joy, faith and hope! Such is the transforming power of the gospel.

Although I spend most of my life traveling the world and publicly preaching the gospel, I am not exempt from the Christian calling to reach out to the people in my world. God's heart will always be for the individual. You and I must never allow ourselves to forsake our personal responsibility toward those in the world God has placed us. God did not call me to be a professional Christian or to act like one when behind a pulpit. I, like you, have been called to *be* a Christian at all times.

A Call to Action

In a world so often characterized by fear, pain and indifference, we hear an incessant cry for help and answers. If we are to reach and influence our world, we must be firmly committed to the process of strengthening our spiritual core so that we can love the Lord our God with all our heart, soul and mind. Only then can we truly love our neighbor as we love ourselves, and only then can we fully possess a genuine, unconditional love for people—a love that will empower us to boldly step into the world, carrying within us a light so bright that it shatters the darkness and confusion.

The world is begging for heroes and crying for freedom. You and I must bring to them the freedom only found through the healing power of Jesus. You and me, a strong army of men and women, refusing to simply *act* like a Christian, but determined to *be* one.

JUST BE ONE

THE ART OF BEING

We have come full circle. I started by saying that we need to stop acting like a Christian and just be one, and have concluded by saying that if we truly are a Christian then we will act like one. There is no doubt that the Bible teaches that Christians should live and act in certain ways, but if these actions do not stem from a strong spiritual core, then we are just acting the part, not living in the fullness of life in Christ. Authentic Christianity is about external actions flowing naturally from an internal life lived in intimacy with our Creator.

I recognize that this concept is not necessarily easy to grasp, and for this reason, I have deliberately shifted gears in the second part of this book. Instead of simply downloading more information for you to digest, I am inviting you on a 31-day interactive journey to discover the art of "being" Christian.

For each of the 31 days, I have highlighted key concepts and allowed space for you to reflect on these. In the book of Psalms, we frequently come across the term *Selah*, which is thought to mean that we should pause and reflect on what has been said. This is exactly what I would love you to do with each thought on the art of "being."

It would be so easy to just close this book right now and move on to the next thing, but I encourage you to keep reading. A key to becoming who we are supposed to be in Christ is to pause long enough in our overscheduled and hectic lives to spend time in His presence, allowing ourselves to be conformed to His image. I would love you to commit a portion of time each day to reflect on the thoughts I have highlighted. I have intentionally presented one thought per day over the span of one month so that you can develop (or maintain) the habit of making time to be with Jesus daily. In 2 Corinthians 3:18, Paul writes, "But we all, with unveiled face, beholding as in a mirror the glory of the Lord, are being transformed into the same image from glory to glory, just as by the Spirit of the Lord." Lasting transformation can only take place in the presence of God.

So, grab a cup of coffee, tea, hot chocolate, juice or water (add lemon) and a notebook or journal. It's time to *Selah*!

BE: WHOLE

Just as our physical core is responsible for every move our body makes, so our spiritual core is responsible for our every thought, emotion, reaction and decision.

I had a friend who wanted to make those fine laugh lines appear less embedded in her cheeks, so she went to get a tube of anti-wrinkle cream. Wanting to stay within her frugal budget, she grabbed one of the more inexpensive brands—it had fancy packaging that claimed to reduce wrinkles by some insane percentage, so she bought it. A few days later (or I should say a few pimples and dry patches later), she realized that this cream contained no real anti-aging ingredients. The packaging had all been a gimmick!

Seeing my friend's blotchy face after a few applications of that phony lotion reminded me of the importance of having a strong spiritual core. If our core doesn't have the proven "God ingredients," then we're never going to have anything except a flawed Christianity wrapped up in fancy packaging.

We have to stop and take a good look inside ourselves to see what the condition of our core is. So many times, we build layers around our inner core to protect ourselves. We cover ourselves with all sorts of fancy packaging—all the Christian behaviors we know we are "supposed" to have. Eventually we get so good at hiding that we actually believe our own marketing campaign—we have completely forgotten that we even *have* a spiritual core!

We must embark on the process of carefully peeling back the layers to expose our core, because if there is to be any real change in our lives, it must start from the inside out. The whole direction of our lives and the outworking of our destinies flow from here! We cannot *act* our way to our future. In fact, unless we are transformed into the image of Christ, we *have* no future.

The only way to lay hold of the purposes of God for our life is to become who we need to be on the inside. It's only then that we will be able to do what we have been called to do.

Selah

- When you stop to evaluate the state of your spiritual core, are you aware of which areas are weak and which are strong?

- In what situations do you tend to hide behind your outward Christian behaviors?

- In what situations do you find it natural to operate truly from your core?

- What things might be holding you back from trusting God and allowing Him to completely transform your core?

BE: CHRISTLIKE

If we simply try to imitate Christ's external behavior—being kind, compassionate and merciful without strengthening our spiritual core— then we risk missing out on the very process that makes us Christlike.

When I first became a Christian, I found it so amazing to read about all the miraculous signs and wonders Jesus performed during His short time in ministry. Many people were healed, delivered and, on more than one occasion, over 5,000 were fed! If He lived today, Hollywood would be begging Him to star in their next superhero movie. I can just see it now: famous designers creating a Lycra tunic with a big *M* for Messiah across the chest.

As I matured in my faith, I began to understand something that made these accounts truly remarkable: It was *compassion*, nothing more and nothing less, that undergirded every single thing Jesus did. He never performed a miracle for the purpose of showing off His amazing superpowers, thereby building His ministry faster—He simply loved people and was compelled by compassion each day He walked on Earth. He brought deliverance to the demonic, He raised the widow's son from the dead and He broke Jewish laws by reaching out to touch the "unclean" lepers, simply because He was motivated by pure love.

Jesus had a perfectly strong inner core, and every work He performed externally naturally flowed from who He was internally. He never had to struggle to try to be the Son of God—He simply *was*. His deeds were an extension of who He was in His core.

For you and me, being Christlike is not only about our external actions, including things like feeding the poor and helping the marginalized and oppressed. It is also about the condition of our spiritual core and the motives of our heart. We can do all of the right things, but if we are not becoming more like Christ *from the inside out* and allowing these actions to spring from true compassion, then we are not being truly Christlike.

Selah

- When you think about imitating Jesus, what is the first thing that comes to mind? Do you think about reproducing His actions, or do you consider His inner motives and attitude?

- What do the Gospels teach us about the motives of Jesus' heart, soul and mind? Why did He perform all of those miracles anyway?

- What does *being* a Christian really mean to you?

- Based on the way you are living your Christian life today, do you think that becoming Christlike is your primary goal?

- Read Luke 7:11-17. Consider what moved the heart of Jesus before He preformed the miracle. Are you filled with this same compassion?

BE: A PILGRIM

*Essentially, we become actors in a drama rather than pilgrims on
a journey. We try to act like something we are supposed to be.*

Some of us live our life as if it were a dress rehearsal for another
life in another time. Jacques in Shakespeare's *MacBeth* says, "All
the world's a stage, and all the men and women merely players;
they have their exits and their entrances, and one man in his time
plays many parts." As romantic as this sounds, we must remember that you and I are not actors pretending to be Christians in
the drama of life. We are on a very real journey to Christlikeness,
and we cannot "perform" our way into becoming like Him.

Every interaction that we have *every day* is part of this pilgrimage. This includes the ways in which we respond to the circumstances we face, the kindness we choose to have, the irritations we
choose to hang on to and the generosity we choose to operate in.
All the challenges and joys of life are part of the process of helping
us to be conformed and transformed to the image of Christ.

I grew up in a strict Greek Orthodox home and remember
being told each Sunday, "Christine, you better behave in church
because God is watching you!" I soon learned that if I ever wanted

to have "fun," I had to do it when I was not at church or any other Christian activity. As a result, my life became compartmentalized, and I put on an Emmy Award-winning performance as "Christian Christine" for a few hours every Sunday. During the rest of the week, I was the real me and lived the way I wanted.

It was only when I truly surrendered my heart to Jesus that I realized that He was with me in every circumstance, each day, and not just for a few hours on a Sunday. It changed the way I live my life. Now I understand that everything matters and that God is with me everywhere. My Christian journey is not about some far away destination but is worked out in the details of my everyday life. If I view my life as a pilgrimage, I intentionally see every moment as an opportunity to become more like Jesus, rather than waiting for carefully selected hours in my life when I take the stage and act like Him.

Selah

- Have you ever found yourself acting like a Christian when you knew on the inside it was a different story?

- If you truly believed that Jesus was with you 24 hours a day, seven days a week, would you change the way that you think or act in any area of your life? If so, what areas?

- Is the "you" that people see at church the same "you" that people know at home, work, college, etc?

- Read 1 Peter 2:11-12 and consider what a life committed to pilgrimage really looks like.

BE: GENEROUS

*Strengthening our spiritual core is not just for our benefit—
it's also for the benefit of others. Remember, God has
called us to love Him and to love others.*

"Mine!"

When my daughter Catherine was about two, she had many words she was able to communicate, but whenever we would have another toddler over to play at the house, there seemed to be only one word in her vocabulary: "Mine!" The guest could have ventured to the very bottom of the toy chest and picked out something Catherine had not played with for months, but as soon as she saw it in another child's hands . . . well, you know: "Mine!"

All children go through this phase, and it takes another year or two for them to sincerely want to share their toys. With the right direction, they begin to grasp the concept that they are not the center of the universe—that every other human being has *not* been placed here for their pleasure and convenience.

When many of us became saved, we had so much negative junk in our soul that we needed to spend that first season as

Christians focused on healing and renewing our spiritual core. This isn't a bad thing at all, unless we get comfortable and stay there. There comes a time when we must not only focus on our own spiritual wholeness, but we must also begin to reach out to the world around us.

Becoming a Christian does not mean we join a private and exclusive club. On the contrary, Jesus invites us to be part of an inclusive community in which we love our neighbor as we love ourselves. Christianity is loving God *and* loving other people.

It would be ridiculous to think about a person standing in front of her church, guarding the front doors and yelling, "Mine!" to any new person trying to enter. Or someone else running to pull another away from going down to receive Jesus at the altar, pointing up to heaven and saying, "Mine!" We would think there was something seriously wrong with that person—but if we are brutally honest, don't we sometimes think this way? Some of us don't *really* want our church to grow to the point that we have to wake up earlier in order to get a good seat and parking place. Some of us have looked at the attire of the person coming down to receive Jesus and thought, *That person is never going to fit in here—what if he tries to steal my purse next Sunday?*

The Church does not exist to satisfy each and every one of our selfish pursuits and ambitions, but rather it is a place where we can serve the needs of others. I think Rick Warren summed it up perfectly in the opening line of his book *The Purpose Driven Life*: "It's not about you."[1]

Selah

- What are some things that hinder you from being "others" focused?

- When you walk into a café, do you see the person behind the counter as someone who is there just to make your coffee, or do you see him or her as a *real* person, someone Jesus loves just as much as He loves you?

- Is there someone in your life who needs to be loved by you and yet you have avoided him or her? What can you do to reach out to this person?

- Are you gracious and welcoming to new people you meet, or would someone be hesitant to approach you?

- Read John 13:34-35. According to Jesus, by what will people be known as His disciples?

Note

1. Rick Warren, *The Purpose Driven Life* (Grand Rapids, MI: Zondervan, 2003).

BE: RELATIONAL

Jesus did not die so that we could have a religious belief system but rather a life-giving relationship with our Father.

When I watch Nick interact with our daughters, I am often moved to tears by his tenderness, love, delight, generosity, protection and provision. Nick is not detached, aloof, distant or rigid with the girls; rather, he is involved with them and their *whole* lives. If Catherine comes to her daddy to share with him the newest outfit she just got for her doll or to show him her most recent work of art, he always responds with genuine interest and excitement. Even if he thinks the doll's dress looks identical to the rest of her wardrobe or he cannot make out which of her drawings is him and which one is the dog, he knows these things are important to Catherine. That makes them important to him.

The most wonderful aspect of Nick's love for the girls is the fact that it's *unconditional*. He does not expect the girls to do anything for him to merit his affection—he is simply besotted with them for who they are. His devotion is not forced or manufactured; it just bursts forth from his heart of love. This is *exactly* how God the Father loves us! It's such a blessing for me to see this, because it took many years for me to know I could have a personal relationship with God like the one Nick shares with our daughters.

I'm sure it must grieve God to have paid such a great price for our salvation and freedom only to find so many still shackled by the bondage of religion. He does not want us to try to relate to Him through tedious ritual or religious protocol, but rather to enter boldly into His throne room of grace, full of joy and expectation.

Dare to open up your heart and life to the freedom of a relationship with your heavenly Father! Perhaps your experience with your earthly father was negative or nonexistent, but you must not allow yourself to believe that who he was or how he felt about you is in any way a reflection of God. God loves you and longs for an intimate relationship with you.

Selah

- How do you see God? Is He a reflection of your earthly father? Is He a strong disciplinarian? Is He angry, distant and aloof? Is He fun-loving and caring?

- How do you think your perception of God has impacted your relationship with Him?

- Do you believe God is interested in every detail of your life, so much that you can trust Him with your deepest, most intimate thoughts, dreams and fears? In what ways can you become more open, vulnerable and intimate with God?

- Read Matthew 7:7-11. How does this passage of Scripture describe God the Father? Is this the way that you relate to God?

BE: INTIMATE

Christians often leave their first love, Jesus, because they have allowed their faith to become a boring ritual rather than a breathtakingly intimate relationship with Him.

Have you ever been at a restaurant and noticed how many couples sit at their tables and barely ever say a word to each other? Sometimes the wife will say more words to the waitress than she does to her husband the entire evening! Being Greek and a woman, I cannot even fathom this behavior! Certainly there is *something* to say—how his day went, how her hair looks, even how she likes the new brand of toothpaste he bought . . . *something*!

I love my husband and am so glad we are committed to never develop any old-people, boring-rut routines. After all these years of marriage, Nick still manages to surprise me and express his love for me in many different ways. He calls me several times a day for no other reason than to tell me he loves me, and he buys me small gifts and leaves them for me to find. And my personal favorite: He helps with the housework and the daily care of our girls (yes, acts of service are my love language!).

We are determined to keep our relationship a spontaneous, fun adventure, because we know this will help us to remain happily married.

We also consciously choose to do the same with our relationship with God. I would hate to find myself spending time with God and feel like I had nothing to say to Him except some awkward banter: "So, uh, what's new, God? Seen any good movies lately? Uh, have you heard the one about the priest, the minister and the rabbi walking into a bar . . ."

Selah

· Have your devotional times lately been like an awkward or boring date with God, or have they been intimate and full of life?

· When you talk to God, can He get a word in edgewise?

· What is one thing you can do today to help put the spark back into your relationship with Jesus?

· Can you remember the last time you spontaneously prayed to God for no other reason than to tell Him you love Him?

· In Matthew 6:9-13 Jesus teaches us how to pray to the Father. Is this prayer reflective of your personal time with God?

BE: GRATEFUL

*To keep our hearts alive and vibrant, we need to maintain
an attitude of gratitude and thanksgiving.*

I clearly remember the first Sunday night I walked into our church and my breath was taken away. The warehouse was jam-packed with people praising God, and I could see the passion and devotion in their faces. None of the teenagers resembled how *I* had approached church at their age: trying to find any excuse not to be there. I had never heard such amazing music, as I came from a church that had no time for any instruments or congregational singing amid all the chanting and incense burning. I could not believe that the message preached was (1) from the Bible, (2) in a language I could actually understand, and (3) made sense and could be applied to my life!

As I can never do anything halfway, I immediately signed up to become a part of a small group, to volunteer in the youth group, to attend the 6 A.M. prayer meeting, to be in the evangelism team—I wanted to live this life of worship to the fullest. I was so grateful to God that such an awesome church so full of life, vibrancy and hope even *existed*. Now, almost two decades later, I have to say I am *still* grateful.

I am grateful to God that I am saved, that He has brought an amazing husband into my life, and that He has given me awesome children, friends, church and a purpose. Each time I get on a plane to go to a conference, I still give thanks for the opportunity to preach the gospel. I have determined that I will never get to the place where I find myself thinking, *Oh, here we go, another sermon. Wow, are we singing that song again? I have heard my pastor tell that joke a hundred times.* In the same way, I am not going to take my family, friends or church for granted.

Often the longer we walk with God, the more familiar we become with Him and His Word. If we are not careful, before we know it, we are no longer grateful—and if we are not doing the activities of being a Christian from the overflow of a grateful heart, acting like Christians is just around the corner.

Selah

- Do you think that you may have become familiar with God or the things of God? In your own life, what signs can you identify that are evidence of this?

- What practical steps can you take in your spiritual journey to ensure that familiarity does not breed contempt in your relationship with God?

- Why not start right now by thanking God for three things in your life?

- Read Luke 17:11-19. What does this story show you about the consequences of gratitude?

BE: CONTENT

*Lust is when we have a desire for something
that is not ours to have.*

Children are so much fun to watch because they shamelessly demonstrate many aspects of human nature, while we adults have learned to cleverly mask the socially unacceptable ones. Two aspects I see often in my girls are *comparison* and *lust*.

Human nature is such that we spend much of our time focusing on what it is that we do *not* have and on what someone else *does* have. Catherine and Sophia each have many different toys, but I can guarantee the only one each wants is the one the other is holding. Catherine can be sitting surrounded by 27 toys, and Sophia only one—and *that* is the one Catherine desperately needs to complete her collection.

I work with them, teaching them to be satisfied with what they have and trying to help them to stop comparing. As Christians, we must learn this same lesson. God has a great plan and purpose for each one of us and has given each many gifts and talents, but so often we are like Catherine, sitting surrounded by all our gifts but focusing on and desiring the talent someone else has.

This is lust, and if we allow ourselves to become distracted by it, we will miss out on the only destiny that will bring us deep satisfaction.

God desires for us to live with a deep contentment in our hearts, but we can only experience this when we embrace *His* plan for our lives. There is no use desiring to be a worship leader and lusting after that position or title if God has not ordained that for your life. If you cannot hold a tune or you are tone deaf, it is highly unlikely that your calling is to be a worship leader. We've all seen these kinds of people on *American Idol* . . . don't be one of them! The only reward you will get from trying to live out someone else's destiny is contention and dissatisfaction. We must keep our eyes focused on Jesus and learn to love and be content with His plan and purpose for our life.

Selah

- Can you think of any area in your own life where you may be desiring something that God does not have for you?

- Can you see how your gifts and abilities are connected to the dreams that God has placed in your heart?

- Are there recurring things that take your focus away from Jesus and His plan for your life?

- Read Hebrews 12:1-2. What does this passage show us about the key to running our own race and finishing our course?

BE: PREPARED

God has a plan for each one of us, and we must do our part to see that plan realized.

Lauren was jamming a piece of toast down her throat while simultaneously buttoning her shirt and shoving her feet into her shoes. She was late for work—again. Today of all days was not the day to be late. She was scheduled to give a presentation that, if it was selected, would mean a huge promotion. This was the opportunity she had been believing God for, and Lauren was confident she would have His favor on her as she pitched her new ideas to her boss.

God, please make there be no traffic today, she prayed, *and thanks for giving me this promotion. I realize I'm late for the fourteenth time this month, but please give my boss Your grace for me as I present today. Also, can You make him forget about how I didn't get that project done last week and had to have someone else cover for me? Oh, yeah, and the one the week before, too. And while You're at it, can You help him to understand that I am a creative person and to keep my workspace clean every moment of the day inhibits my creativity? What's the big deal if I have piles all over my desk?*

Even with all of her prayers, I seriously doubt that Lauren is going to get that promotion. Many people think that just because they are Christians, God is going to drop their destiny out of the sky like fairy dust. Somehow, it is going to materialize with little effort on their part.

Nothing could be farther from the truth! We must understand that fulfilling our destiny is all up to God—*and* all up to us. We must partner *with* Him in order to become who we need to be so that we can do all that He has called us to do.

Selah

- Are you expecting God to magically zap you into your destiny?

- In what ways does your "God will take care of it" attitude manifest itself?

- Outline a few practical steps that will help make your relationship with God a partnership.

- In Matthew 25:14-30, we find that two servants were considered good and faithful, and the other wicked. What is the reason for this distinction? Are you doing all you can with what is in your hand today to fulfill the purpose of God tomorrow?

BE: OBEDIENT

*Whatever it is, we must remember that every small step
of obedience has eternal ramifications.*

As we were hurriedly being shuttled from one airport terminal in
Frankfurt to the other, I looked across the crowded bus and
noticed one particular elderly couple. They looked fearful—I knew
that they must be worried that they were not going to make their
flight. Our plane had arrived very late, and it was likely that many
of us on the bus would miss our connecting flights. I noticed that
the couple could not speak English or German, and I saw their
boarding pass was for Istanbul. *They are Turkish,* I thought to
myself, *and they have no idea what's going on.*

As I looked back at Nick and the girls to see how they were
faring on this squished and bumpy bus, I heard God's still, small
voice within me say, *You need to help that couple.* I almost answered
out loud, "God, how can I help them? Their plane leaves from
another terminal—I will miss my plane, and I have to preach in
Stockholm tonight. What about Nick and the girls?" His only
response was, *Help that couple get to their plane.* I only had a split
second to decide.

"Nick," I said, "you take the girls and go—give me my pass-
port and pray that I make it."

I walked over to the couple, who must have been in their 80s, at least. I gently took them by the hand and walked them to their gate. The woman was so thankful that she began to sob as we walked. When we arrived at their gate, she looked at me, patted my face and kissed me, thanking Allah for sending me to them. Suddenly, I got the full picture of what God was doing. In that instant, I was able to look into her eyes, smile and whisper, "Jesus Christ loves you."

She stopped and looked at me, began to cry some more, and then disappeared onto the plane.

I felt so humbled and honored to be a part of God's beautiful invitation for this couple to know Him. What seemed at first like a hassle to me became a once-in-a lifetime moment to sow a seed. Imagine the opportunity I would have missed had I not been obedient.

Selah

- Can you think of a time when you did not respond obediently to the prompting of God? How did you feel after the opportunity had passed you by?

- Why do you think we find it so difficult to obey God?

- Why don't you make the decision today to do the thing that you know God is asking you to do? (For example, send that note of encouragement, make that apology, sign up for Bible school, etc.)

- Read the book of Jonah and meditate on the consequences of disobedience. Consider whether there is any area in your life that you have been running from God.

BE: LOVED

I just could not get my eyes off those last four words:
"He delighted in me."

From the time Catherine started formulating sentences, she has asked, "Mummy, can you come and play with me?" or "Mummy, can you read me a book?" I always reply, "Yes! That is one of my greatest pleasures in life!" As a result, I now have a little girl who is convinced at the very core of who she is that her mummy loves spending time with her, listening to her stories, watching her twirl at dance classes and talking through any questions she might have. (And I get to do it all over again with Sophia!)

I truly delight in her, in everything about her, not just in what she does—there are definitely things she does that I do not delight in. I am captivated and besotted simply by who she is and who she is becoming. I am so happy that she is entirely confident in the devotion that Nick and I have for her, because this is an area of life that I struggled with for many years. I found it very difficult to believe that *anyone* would actually delight in me simply for who I am. I saw myself as not good enough, not smart enough, not cool enough, not *anything* enough.

It took me a very long time to renew my mind and to truly believe that in the same way I love my precious daughters—totally head over heels for no other reason than the fact they breathe air—God loves me. Just as I love their personalities, little quirks, laughter, dimples, cute questions, so too God loves *me* purely, totally and unconditionally, simply because He made me and is my Father. God delights in *all* of His children . . . God delights in *you*.

Selah

- Do you really believe that God delights in you? Not in what you do or how much you accomplish, but in *you*? If not, why?

- Can you remember a time when you did not feel "enough" to be loved and chosen by God? How did this affect your relationship with God?

- Are you too busy doing things for God to simply stop and bask in His presence, love and delight?

- Make a list of what God says about you, His child, in His Word, and meditate on these Scriptures daily.

- Read Psalm 139 and meditate on the love of God and how precious you are to Him.

BE: TRANSFORMED

If our soul is damaged or wounded before we become a Christian, it isn't miraculously "zapped"—we aren't instantly made whole.

I have been a runner for more than 20 years, and a while ago, I noticed each time I ran I'd get a sharp pain in my right hip. At first, I just ignored it because I couldn't be bothered to get it checked out. However, the pain became so intense that I had no choice but to visit a physiotherapist—which was better than going on record as the youngest recipient of an artificial hip replacement.

At my first visit, I said (in true Christine style), "Can we deal with this quickly? I have a half-marathon coming up, and I need it to be healed by then." After he examined me, he laughed and said, "Christine, your entire hip and all the surrounding muscles have been totally damaged. It's taken years of poor form and lack of stretching for it to get like this—it's going to take a long time for it to heal. There isn't going to be a half, quarter or any portion of a marathon this year."

It took almost a year of constant therapy for the pain to subside and my hip to be healed. Because I committed the time needed for the healing process and because I was open to learning new patterns of exercise and stretching, my hip is better than ever. Now I'm confident I'll be able to run for many decades to come.

Having a truly prosperous soul happens the same way. It has often taken years for our soul to become damaged and deeply wounded, and there is a process involved in making it whole. We'd love for this change to happen overnight, but God's ways cannot be compared to a microwave—He operates much more like a crock-pot! We must commit to the internal healing process for God's restoration to take place, because an artificial soul replacement is simply not an option. We have to work with what we've been given. But don't worry—God is faithful and will bring healing if we are willing to commit to His plan and His process.

Selah

- What pre-Christian soul damage is affecting your current Christian walk?

- Are there any recurring behavior patterns you have been trying to address from the outside in, but which have their origin in a wounded soul?

- Is there any area of your life in which you started on a path to healing, but you got frustrated and decided to give up?

- What areas of your life have you been waiting for God to "zap" to bring instant wholeness to?

- In 3 John 2, John prays that we have a prosperous soul. How would you describe a soul that is prospering?

BE: FRUITFUL

There was nowhere in the Bible where I could find a Scripture that said, "By their gifts you will know them" (trust me, I searched the whole Bible).

Remember in grade school when we played sports at recess? Two kids would be appointed as captains for each team, and the rest of us nervously stood there, hoping that we wouldn't be the last one picked. I think that was when most of us first began to notice that popularity was closely linked to the kinds of gifts and talents we possess. We learned that if we had all the "right stuff" (looks, charisma, talent, and so on), we would be able to be part of the "in" crowd—and if we didn't, we were banished to the geek table at lunch.

You just need to turn on the TV or buy a magazine to see that we live in a society that celebrates and exalts people who are gifted and talented. Our media bombards us with images of the greatest athletes, actors and rock stars whom they deem to be the most beautiful, famous and intelligent. The public will even excuse shortcomings these "idols" might have, such as a string of failed marriages, immoral behavior, substance abuse, lack of self-control, and pride. Despite their failings, these people are still considered role models.

As Christians, we cannot allow ourselves to fall into the trap of being enamored by someone purely on the basis of his or her gift or talent. A person's spiritual gifting does not define who that person is. We need to examine the *fruit* of a person's life to truly determine his or her character. Certainly, every one of us is unique and special to God and has God-given gifts and talents, but it is the fruit of our lives that truly reveals the depth of our intimacy with the Father. It is when we are in His presence that we are changed into His likeness and consequently produce the fruits of His Holy Spirit.

Let's resolve to focus on developing the fruits of love, joy, peace, patience, kindness, goodness, faithfulness, gentleness and self-control. These are the measure of our Christlikeness.

Selah

- When you look at others, do you only look at their gifts— or do you look beyond, to their character?

- Whom do you consider to be a role model? Why? What qualities do you admire in that person?

- Do you think that other people see any fruits of the Spirit in your life?

- Choose one of the fruits of the Spirit, and think of an area of your life in which this fruit may be lacking. How can you allow God to develop this particular fruit in this area?

- Read Matthew 7:15-20. In this passage of Scripture, what does Jesus teach us about the fruit of our lives?

BE: AUTHENTIC

*If the gifts of the Spirit on a person's life are greater
than the fruit of the Spirit in a person's life,
parts of that life will begin to crumble.*

One of my friends in college was one of those people who seemed to have a Midas touch—everything that he touched turned to gold. Martin had a charisma about him, and every person who met him was naturally drawn to him. He was the whole package: good-looking, athletic, very bright and a dynamic speaker. No one was surprised when he made law his career of choice, and he breezed through college, followed by a Master's Degree in law, without needing to study much at all.

While Martin appeared to have it all together, we had many long talks throughout college about his desperate desire to be accepted by his father—he felt that nothing he did was ever good enough, and this was his biggest motivation for always being the best. Martin was one of the most popular guys I knew at college, and he always threw the best parties on campus, but underneath his "perfect" life, he was riddled with insecurity and a desperate need for affirmation and approval.

Upon graduation, Martin was courted by several prestigious law firms, all of which ensured that he and his new wife would be starting out on an unbelievable salary. It appeared as if every part of his life was coming together perfectly. In only a few years, he was climbing the ranks within the company, becoming very wealthy and being considered for a promotion. About that time, however, many of Martin's colleagues developed a habit of getting "casually high," (as they called it) and with Martin's desperation to be accepted and popular, it wasn't long before his six-figure salary afforded him a full-blown addiction to cocaine.

Soon he was finding it harder and harder to make it to work on Mondays, and almost as hard to wait until Friday to begin his drug binge. His wife wanted to start having children, but she was beginning to doubt Martin's fidelity (and with good reason). On the day he found out that he didn't get the promotion, he came home to find that his wife had left him, along with most of their possessions. Faster than it took to rise to the top, Martin's life came crashing down around him.

The condition of Martin's inner world was starting to be revealed by the collapse of his external world. It is always dangerous when our gifts take us to a place where our character cannot keep us.

Selah

• What are the primary gifts that you think God has given you?

• Are there areas in your life where there is an inconsistency between your inner and outer life?

• Do you think that the current condition of your inner core is strong enough to sustain the kind of life that God has gifted you for?

• Do you have an accountability group or somebody in your life to help keep you on track? If so, are you honest, open and vulnerable with them?

BE: BRAINWASHED

In short, if we want to change our life, we must change the way we think.

As you are already aware, after I gave birth to Sophia, I was determined to lose the extra pounds I had gained while pregnant. Being somewhat extreme, I emptied my house of all traces of unhealthy food and stocked my refrigerator and cupboards with every variation of lettuce that exists, as well as soups and vegetables. I did not venture beyond a two-mile radius of my home so that I would not be tempted to stop at my favorite ice cream shop. I was determined to lose weight— I thought that being healthy meant being able to fit back into my favorite jeans.

Finally I relented and agreed to catch up with two friends at a local restaurant. When the waiter came to take our order, I was determined to stick to my new eating regimen, so I ordered a salad with no cheese, no croutons, fat-free dressing on the side and a glass of hot water with lemon. My friends commented on how great I looked and that they too needed to change their eating habits.

About 10 minutes into our conversation, an appetizer of potato skins arrived. They looked divine! Then came the chocolate shakes, and the main courses of ribs for one friend, bacon alfredo for another—followed by my dry, cheeseless, croutonless salad. I started fidgeting in my seat and had to concentrate on keeping my mouth shut in order to stop myself from drooling. The tempting aroma of all this amazing food drifted past my nose as I slowly tried to chew the weeds on my tiny plate.

Halfway through the meal, my friends excused themselves to use the restroom. As soon as they were gone, I dug in. I knew that I only had a few minutes, so I acted fast. I stuffed a few ribs in my mouth, washed them down with chocolate shake and spun a forkful of alfredo noodles so thick that I almost got lockjaw trying to fit it in. I emptied the leftover potato skins into my purse, slid the plate under the table (I could say the waiter took them) and wiped my mouth just in time to welcome my friends back to the table. If they noticed the missing food, they never mentioned it, and I finished off my weeds feeling a bit defeated.

This little episode taught me a lesson: My thoughts about being healthy were not about the type of food that I ate, but rather about losing weight. Because I did not have a healthy mind-set, I was kidding myself if I thought I was going to be able to keep up a healthy diet. My brain needed to be "washed" and renewed before my habits could be modified.

Selah

- Is there an area in your life in which you need to renew, or "wash," your mind with the Word of God?

- Can you identify any areas in your life in which you changed your behavior but not the way you thought about your behavior? If so, did you find that you eventually relapsed?

- Can you identify thoughts you have about yourself or others that are contrary to God's thoughts?

- What can you start to do today to begin to renew your mind?

- Read Romans 12:2 and consider how true transformation occurs.

BE: INTENTIONAL

Our thoughts are just like a train; they always take us somewhere.

"Honey, don't you worry about a thing; everyone is going to adore you." Yet even as I said this to Catherine, I could tell she was not the least bit concerned. It was her first day at school, and I was taking her to class by the hand, quite pleased about how calm I felt. *This is going to be a breeze*, I thought. *Why do other mums make such an emotional ordeal of the first day of school? It's just the next step in the normal growing-up process.*

As we approached the door, however, I had this strange unsettling feeling happening inside me, and when it came time for me to let go of Catherine's hand, I couldn't seem to uncurl my fingers. I had the thought, *Maybe this wasn't such a good idea. Maybe Catherine isn't ready yet.* Then Catherine said, "Mummy, you will be okay. I will be home this afternoon, and now I want to go and play with my friends. Goodbye." Without waiting for me to reply, my five-year-old let go of my hand and did not even look back as she went to the playground to find some new friends.

I watched her skip off and the "what ifs" began: *What if she doesn't get along with the other girls? What if she can't do the schoolwork? What if she needs me in the middle of the day and I'm not here?* And so it went for about 10 minutes as I played out different scenarios in my mind. I could only come to one conclusion: My daughter as an adult will require serious therapy as a result of her mother abandoning her to the school system. *I should offer to pay for that,* I thought—and then I came to my senses. What was I thinking?!

As absurd as my story sounds, I'm sure you have experienced something like it. At times we have all allowed our thoughts to travel down a random track and end up concluding ridiculously negative scenarios that will never actually happen. Just like I had to do, standing on the playground, we must "come to our senses," take control of our thoughts and begin to think as God would think! If we resolve to keep getting on the *right* train of thought, we will always get off at the right destination. The choice is ours—let's make the most of it!

Selah

- Think of one challenge in your life right now. Where are your thoughts about it taking you? Are you headed for a train wreck?

- Can you think of any "platforms" you need to stay away from, as there always seem to be trains passing by that are headed in the wrong direction?

- List three things that help you choose the right trains of thought.

- For the next 24 hours, *think* about what you are *thinking about*—you might be shocked!

BE: DETERMINED

It is only during times of trials that the true strength of our mind muscle is revealed. What is in us will always flow out of us during these times.

There are certain moments in life that define us, that reveal the level of spiritual maturity to which we have grown and that sometimes alter our lives forever. One of these defining moments in my life occurred when I was 33 years old. Standing in my mother's kitchen, I found out for the first time that I was not who I thought I was. The parents whom I had always known as "Mum" and "Dad" were not in fact my biological parents. And every *fact* that I had thought to be true about my background, heritage and life was not actually so.

Finding out that I was adopted happened so suddenly and unexpectedly that I had no time to consult the Bible about what I should think. At that moment, my identity was challenged at the very core of my being, and this challenge exposed what was really inside of me—what I *truly* thought and believed. One of the first things I said aloud that day was, "Well, before I was formed in my mother's womb—He knew me."

I have to say that, after the shock of this news wore off, I felt joy in my heart at my response. I had so renewed my mind with the Word of God that I had been totally transformed, and even though at that moment the enemy tried to make me think that I was an accident and had no intrinsic worth or value, I knew better. As a result of having saturated my mind with the Word of God for years, in that defining moment, I believed the *truth* of who I really was, over the facts of where I came from.

Sometimes we think that we react a certain way because of the adversity that we confront. The truth is that the challenges we encounter merely reveal who we really are.

Selah

- Do you tend to let your circumstances dictate your thoughts, or does the Word of God determine how you think?

- Do you keep a list of the promises from God's Word that are specifically for you? If not, take some time to write them down, and reflect upon them regularly.

- Think of a challenge you are currently facing. Now pick up your Bible and find a Scripture that speaks truth into your difficulty. When you are tempted to be discouraged, hold on to that truth!

- Read Matthew 8:5-13. How did the centurion respond to the grave condition of his servant? Why was the servant ultimately healed? What lessons can you learn from this story?

BE: GENUINE

Loving God is only the beginning of being an authentic Christian.

My Nick is a romantic through and through. When he proposed to me, he offered me one of the most gorgeous diamond rings I had ever seen. It was an original ring with a unique design, and he was quick to point out the gold and the diamonds (yes, diamonds, *plural*—he's the man!). I found out later that he had worked an entire year from 11 P.M. to 3 A.M. while in Bible college in order to be able to provide the real deal.

I was certainly not an expert in fine diamonds: Nick could have easily given me a cheap substitute and I wouldn't have known—at first. As time went by, however, a fake wouldn't have endured the rigors of daily wear. The fake gold would have begun to chip off, and it would have started to leave a green ring around my finger at some point. Even I would have realized that the ring was not what I thought it was. I would have seen that it was just a sham, an imitation, just like the jewelry I played with as a child.

We recently had the ring refurbished. When the jeweler looked at the ring more closely, he commented on how beautiful the stone was, what a well-crafted cut the diamond had and just how valuable the ring was.

We are supposed to be just like that: the genuine article, "real deal" Christians. When people get to know us up close and personal, they should be able to see that we are on the inside what we profess to be on the outside—not a cheap substitute.

The people around us can tell whether we are genuine Christians, not from how much we profess to love God, but from how we love our neighbor as we love ourselves. As loving God is only the beginning of being an authentic Christian, we must extend this love in a very tangible and practical way to those in our world. Truly, they will know we are Christians by our love.

Selah

- Do you think it's possible to love God and not love other people?

- Why is loving God the beginning and not the end of our Christianity if it is the "greatest commandment"?

- Can you live a life filled with Christian "works" and still not be an authentic Christian? Why or why not?

- Can you be an authentic Christian while neglecting the work Christ has called you (and me) to do? Why or why not?

- Read Matthew 23:25-28 and reflect on how earnestly Jesus desires that we are authentic at our core.

BE: THE CHURCH

*A church loses its life and effectiveness at the point it stops
being the church that God created her to be and starts
going through the motions of doing church.*

When I was in school, we studied the play *Shirley Valentine* by
Willy Russell. It was about a wisecracking, completely unpre-
dictable English housewife who was totally bored with her sub-
urban life. Her life had become one boring routine of getting
her husband off to work and helping the kids through school.
During the day she would methodically complete her list of
routine tasks: the grocery shopping, cooking, ironing and
cleaning. She would go to bed and then get up and begin the
same routine all over again.

One of her most notable quirks consisted of her conversations with the kitchen wall. A large part of the play is in fact a
monologue of Shirley talking to the wall. Alone all day, she
chose to share her thoughts and feelings with the wall as her
only means of companionship. At one point she says, "Most of
us are dead before we die, and the thing that kills us is all of this
unused life we carry around with us."

So many lives are literally like this: We get up and go through our well-rehearsed motions of existence; we check all our tasks off our lists and go to bed; we arise the next day and do it all over again. As Christians, we know that such a mundane existence falls far short of the abundant life Jesus came to give us. God did not create all of us with such creativity, cultural diversity and unique gifts and talents to simply go through the motions of a religious, boring life. As Christians, with the power of the Creator of the Universe inside of us, we should be living the most exciting, exhilarating lives on the planet!

In the same way, a church that is going through the motions of "doing church" has missed the point of what God created her to be. God never intended for His Church to be filled with empty ritual, boring and irrelevant teaching, uninspiring music or a lack of creativity. The Church of Jesus Christ ought to be dynamic, vibrant, life-giving—a place of hope, healing and destiny. Let's be that kind of Church.

Selah

- Do you ever feel like you're just "doing church"? If so, why?

- What are you contributing to your church? (Filling a seat on Sunday doesn't count!)

- Do you think the church exists only to meet your needs?

- Read Matthew 16–18 and describe the kind of Church that you think Jesus is building. What is the kind of Church against which the gates of hell cannot prevail?

DAY 20

BE: SALT

We are the salt of the earth.

I love Greek food. It really is the best in the world, and I'm not just saying that because it is the cuisine of my people. It's simply a fact (at least in my opinion). Much to my delight, I have the opportunity to eat Greek meals in restaurants all over the world because I travel so much; and while some are better than others, they all pale in comparison to the Greek food that is made by the hands of my mum. Her cooking really is the best in the world, and I'm not just saying that because she is my mother. It's simply a fact (at least in my opinion). There just is nothing like her home-cooked moussaka, yemista, taramosalata or Greek salad.

I cannot reveal to you the secret of her recipes that have been handed down for many generations, because then I'd have to kill you. I can, however, share this cooking tip of hers with you: Mum always says, "Christine, the right amount of salt is the definitive factor in the making of every great meal." Too little salt, and the meal is unmemorable and the guests leave full but still unsatisfied. Too much salt, and everyone's lips get that pruned feeling—and the next morning they can't remove the

rings from their hands because their fingers are fat, bloated little sausages. It's hard to get those guests to come back a second
time. Not good.

Jesus told us that we are the salt of the earth, and we need to
ensure that we are deliberately and carefully seasoning the world
around us properly. Too little, and the people with whom we have
relationships leave our presence glad to have seen us, but still feeling unsatisfied in their souls. Too much, and they are repelled—
and it's very difficult to get a second chance to witness to them.

We are all called to bring out the "God flavors" in our part
of the world, and we are each responsible for the "taste" of God
we leave with others.

Selah

- Do people get a good taste of Jesus when they encounter
  you?

- What kind of flavors do you see yourself bringing out
  in your world?

- Take a moment to determine how you can add flavor
  to your world in a positive way today.

- Do you think the example you set as a Christian sometimes errs on the side of being too salty, or not salty
  enough?

- Read Matthew 5:13 in *THE MESSAGE* Bible and evaluate
  whether you are fulfilling God's purpose in your world.

BE: COMPASSIONATE

*We live in a world that often gives more value
to animals, the environment and individual rights than
it does to people, but there is nothing more costly to
God than people. He loves all of us.*

Sitting in my seat on a plane recently, I picked up one of those "shop in the sky" magazines that are filled with every useless gadget known to man. I began to read about the precision portion pet feeder, a programmable feeder that automatically provides exact food portions so that your pets can follow their recommended diet while you are away at work. And I thought, *Thousands of* children *starved to death* today—*how is it that we can allow ourselves to be more concerned that the* pets *of the world get their precise portions?*

Not only did I come across the easy-mount cat door that allows your pet to enter and exit the house unassisted, but also the pet staircase that helps small pets climb up to furniture they could not otherwise reach. I must admit, I laughed out loud as I pictured a miniature hotdog climbing the staircase so that he wouldn't strain his back trying to hop up on the couch. But when I contrasted that picture with the fact that millions of *people* throughout the world had no home at all in which to sleep that night . . . well, the doggie staircase suddenly didn't seem like such a great necessity.

There is nothing wrong with having and loving a pet— that's not at all the point I'm trying to make. But how have we as a society come to a place where we have the resources to research, invent, produce and market such luxuries for our pets and not enough resources to keep human beings alive throughout the world? Again, it's not bad to pamper those we love and to enjoy the little things in life, but if we have forgotten about our fellow man while doing so, we have lost sight of our purpose for being here.

Every single person must be valued and given dignity, because God purposefully gave His Son as a ransom for that person! Let's make sure we are valuing people in the same way that God does: greeting the overwhelmed mummy (the one with three kids in tow!) at the supermarket; extending a hand to help the elderly; looking for people we can bless with our love, our words and our finances. Let's keep our hearts and eyes open to the lost, the hurting and the needy around us and be ready to offer them our generosity!

Selah

- Is there a particular "type" of person you find difficult to value? Why do you think this is so? How can you learn to show compassion for that person?

- Why not seriously consider sponsoring a child (or two) in need—just because you can? (Check out www.com passion.com or www.worldvision.org.)

- Do you pray on a regular basis for your city, your country or for the lost throughout the world? If not, take some time right now to intercede for them.

- Read Romans 5:6-8. What do these verses reveal to us about the kind of people God loves?

BE: A LIGHT

*The strength of our spiritual core actually determines whether we are a
faint flickering candle, a 75-watt light bulb or a stadium spotlight.*

I once spoke at a youth rally in Los Angeles on a typically beautiful, warm Southern California evening. We were having a raucously fun time with over 1,000 teenagers (most of whom were from unchurched backgrounds), rockin' out in the mosh pit as several bands were playing. We were also holding great giveaways as well as skateboarding and basketball competitions, and the church parking lot was abuzz with activity.

The M.C. got the attention of these young people and introduced me as the guest speaker. As I stepped up to the microphone, all the electricity went out. There was no sound and there was no light. Because of the type of event it was, everyone thought this was a gimmick at first, but after several seconds of silent darkness, they all realized that it was an electrical failure. Luckily, the sound came back on very quickly, but we were still in almost complete darkness.

It was very frustrating for me to deliver a message to 1,000 teenagers without being able to see them. The host church eventually brought out dozens of flashlights, which gave enough light to prevent any accidents, but we really needed large floodlights to illuminate the stage and the crowd. Those small battery-powered flashlights were simply incapable of producing enough light, but because of the power shortage and the church's overburdened generator, it was the best we could do.

When it comes to being a light in the world, we have a choice as to how brightly we will shine. If we allow ourselves to become run down and if our spiritual systems begin to operate on low wattage, we will be like those few dozen flashlights trying to illuminate a crowd of 1,000 people. We might be able to help our neighbors enough to steer them away from major mistakes in life, but we won't be able to truly influence their walk. However, if we are diligent and keep our spiritual cores strong and energized, we will be able to operate as a floodlight for Christ, illuminating the way for the people in our world to find the wonderfully abundant life God has planned specifically for them.

Selah

- So many kids stayed in darkness that night because there was not enough light. Are there people in your world who are in darkness because you have not been shining your light bright enough?

- When you do shine, are you more like an intense interrogation light, or a lighthouse on a hill?

· Who do you personally know that is a great example of being a light? Have you allowed that person's example to ignite change in your own life?

· What practical steps can you take to bump up the wattage in the light that shines forth from your life?

· Read John 8:12 and Matthew 5:14. What is it that Jesus says He is and we are? How should this impact the way in which we live our lives?

BE: FOCUSED

*I was defining my Christianity by what I was not doing, completely
forgetting about what it was that I should be doing.*

A typical evening in the Caine household: Nick was taking a
moment to catch up on sports on ESPN and Catherine, my five-
year-old, was upstairs tidying her room before dinner (she was
not allowed to watch *Dora the Explorer* for the zillionth time until
she completed this task). Sophia, my one-year-old, was content-
edly playing in her room, and I was in the kitchen attempting to
accomplish five things at once (as I said, perfectly typical).

I was trying to keep an ear out for what the kids were up to,
cook dinner, set the table, talk on the phone, all the while making last minute changes to this manuscript. It was while I was
typing with one hand and stirring the dinner with the other that
all of a sudden I noticed a strange silence upstairs—the kind that
registers on a mother's radar. I asked Nick, "What is Catherine
doing?" He looked up for a second and listened. "It sounds nice
and quiet—I'm sure she's cleaning her room like you asked."

I wasn't convinced, so I made a quick stir, finished a sentence
on my laptop and went upstairs to take a peek in Catherine's
room. There was my Catie, sitting on the floor painting Sophia's

nails; and from Sophia's moussed hair, blue eyelids and rouged cheeks, I could see my eldest was simply adding her finishing touches to my baby's total makeover. I wanted to bust out laughing but I knew that I would lose all authority if I did, so I put on my best "Mummy Discipline" voice.

"Catherine Bobbie, what are you doing?!" (Middle name usage always means business.) "I told you to clean your room before dinner."

To this she answered innocently, "But Mummy, I didn't turn on Dora."

Catie knew what she was *not* supposed to do—I'll give her that—but she definitely didn't clue in to what she was *supposed* to be doing. So many of us Christians live our lives just like Catherine did that day: We know exactly what we aren't supposed to be doing, but we forget about what we *should be* doing. We *should be* focused on the abundant, purpose-driven, passionate life adventure that we have been called to live. If we maintain this focus, we will not find ourselves getting off track, doing things that we should not be doing. Why? For the simple reason that our lives always move forward in the direction of those things that we're focused on.

Selah

· What are the things you think Christians should *not* do?

· What are the things that Christians *should* do?

· Do you think you focus on what activities you are refraining from, rather than on the things you should be participating in? If so, why?

· What was one of the last things God spoke to you? Is that still your focus, or have you become distracted with something else?

· Read John 10:10 and describe the abundant life for which Jesus came that we might have. What does this kind of life look like for you?

BE: DIFFERENT

I needed to be in her world but not of her world so that through me,
God could bring lasting change to her world.

We often pray that God would use us to help change the world, yet we simultaneously underestimate the opportunities that await us in our everyday life. All of us are in this world (after all, we don't live on Mars), and that means that we have the potential to transform our world one life at a time simply by choosing to *be* Christians in the course of our everyday routine.

When my husband, Nick, was working in the banking industry, his corporate life was very busy and he spent much of his time extremely frustrated because he wanted to be "doing more for God." Then one day an encounter with a colleague made Nick realize that his workplace *was* his mission field.

One of Nick's coworkers, John, had been a professional athlete and was now one of the most successful salesmen in the firm. However, he had recently broken up with his long-time girlfriend, and his personal life was in shambles. One day, he approached Nick and said, "How do you do it?" At first, Nick wasn't sure what John meant because although Nick was also doing well, he was still one of the newer reps. "What do you mean?" Nick asked. "Your life. I mean, you've been here six months, and I've never heard you say one negative thing about anyone. When you talk about your wife, it's clear that you actually love and respect her, and I've never seen you so much as glance at another woman—you won't even *talk* about another woman! At our office parties, you're never the one drunk or out of control. I've never heard you stretch the truth when dealing with a client's finances, and you are the only one on the team who will tell a client not to do a deal if it's not in the client's best interests—and your commissions are still high! How is that? Everyone here loves you and considers you trustworthy, you're always happy, and you've become the go-to guy for anyone here who needs advice. What makes you so different?"

That day Nick realized just how much of an impact he *was* making by simply being a Christian in his workplace. He was in the same world as his colleagues, but very definitely not of that world, and so had the opportunity to impact individual lives with his Christlike example.

Selah

· Do you think of your neighborhood/college/work-place/gym as your mission field?

· What are some examples of ways that you can be in the world but not of the world in those places where you "do life"?

- Have there been times when you realized that you have been both *in* the world and *of* the world? If so, how did you feel?

- If a judge and jury were sent to your home, workplace or neighborhood and put you on trial for being a Christian, would there be enough evidence to convict you?

- Read John 17:14-18. What do you think Jesus is communicating in this passage of Scripture?

BE: ADVANCING

If we have an unfounded fear of the world that causes us to retreat from the world, we will fail to bring light to the world.

I was recently experiencing a bit of sleeplessness on yet another flight across the Atlantic Ocean. My body was tired, but my brain had not decided what time zone it was in yet, so there I was with my eyes open. I began to flip through the movie channels and was instantly drawn to a very moving scene in what looked to be a powerful movie about World War II. In this particular scene, an entire battalion was retreating, under siege from the opposing army, and they were running frantically for their lives.

These men strategically set up another camp, hidden from the enemy, and took the needed time to regroup and recuperate. After a few days, the commander began to rally the troops for retaliation. He expressed that they needed to not only recover the ground they had lost but also charge forward into enemy territory. He delivered a very passionate and motivating speech, but no one moved. This scene seemed to last forever as all the soldiers (save two) sat in awkward silence, refusing to engage in another battle. They had lost their will to fight.

As a group, these troops wanted to stay in this defensive posture until the war was over. Their courage and vision had vanished, and they no longer wanted to risk their lives. Even when they received orders from the commanding headquarters to resume their battle positions, they refused. Some of the army's best men were in this unit, but they had exchanged a mind-set of attack and advance for one of survival and retreat. The commander had big plans for these capable men, but finally, he had to face the fact that these soldiers were now defeated. He said that the men were now peripheral to the mission and no longer central. The result was devastating.

When I saw this, I thought to myself, *Has the Church come to this? Have we retreated from the world and simply set up a defense fortress while we await the rapture?*

We must ensure that we remain actively engaged in the spiritual battle to which we have been enlisted.

Selah

- Have you ever found yourself running from the world? What made you run?

- What is something you consider worth fighting for? Why?

- How is the Church viewed in your world? If it is viewed as irrelevant and withdrawn, what can you do to change that?

- Read 2 Timothy 4:7. How does Paul describe his Christian life in this passage, his farewell address?

BE: A SOLUTION

*The Spirit of the Lord is upon us to enable us to reach out
beyond ourselves and to help others.*

Not long ago, we decided to take Catherine on a trip to South
Africa with us. We thought that it would be good for her to see
how 70 percent of the world's children live and to learn to appre-
ciate just how truly blessed we are as a family.

As we were driving through one of the townships, I could
see Catherine's confusion as she saw the children living on the
side of the road. She was glued to the window of the car, studying every person we passed. "Mummy, why are those girls sleeping on the ground? And how come that boy's shirt is so dirty
and ripped?"

Before I could answer her, she then said, "That girl over there
looks very sad. Can we stop and give her one of my dollies to play
with?" When she later found out that these children didn't go to
school, she said, "I have an idea! Let's just buy them all school
uniforms so that they can go to class!"

As I listened to Catherine's questions, I was reminded of the
purity, innocence and simplicity with which children process

situations. The solution was so simple to Catherine that day—and you know what? In many ways, it *can* be this simple. Imagine what the world would look like if we all considered it our personal responsibility to make a difference in our world. Catherine did not merely highlight the problem, she also offered a solution. Maybe this is one of the reasons Jesus told us to be like little children.

Nick and I are committed to ensuring that our daughters do not grow up oblivious to the needs of the people in their world, even beyond their immediate sphere of influence. We want them to know that they are blessed by God to be a blessing to others. Instead of being daunted by the immense need on the planet, we are determined to be part of the solution by helping to change the world, one life at a time. We cannot do everything to alleviate all of the pain and injustice on the earth, but we must each do something.

You, too, are called to be part of the solution. You are blessed to be a blessing!

Selah

· Can you identify the major needs in your community?

· List some creative ways you or your group can reach out to meet some of these needs.

· What can you do to make yourself more aware of the needs of the people who live on the other side of the world?

- How can you help your friends to not only be more aware of the needs in the world but also to mobilize them to do something about it?

- Read James 1:27; 2:14-20. What do these Scriptures show us about true Christianity?

BE: MEMORABLE

*More than any words, program or doctrine,
it's our very life that speaks the loudest.*

"Excuse me, are you Christine Caryofyllis?"

I was sitting in the hair salon and was very surprised to hear my maiden name. When I spun around in my chair, I was delighted to see Mrs. Jones, one of my high school teachers from 25 years ago! She sat down in the empty chair next to me, and we immediately began sharing what had been happening in our lives over the last quarter century. It was just as easy to talk to her that day as it was when I was a student, and I was very glad to have the opportunity to express to her my appreciation for all she had done for me during those years at school.

She had been an excellent teacher, full of life and joy, and I cannot remember ever going to class and seeing her in a bad mood. She truly believed in all us girls, and she always was available to listen, to encourage and to go out of her way to assist us. I have to admit that I cannot remember anything she taught me in class, but what she taught me about attitude and consideration for other people was invaluable. After all those years, I could still remember the impact she had had on me, as the example of her life had spoken volumes to every one of her students.

The most valuable lesson I learned from Mrs. Jones was this: A person's everyday life speaks louder than 1,000 sermons—and better yet, can still be speaking even after 25 years! Mrs. Jones wasn't an amazing orator, evangelist or pastor. She was simply a woman determined to impact as many lives as she possibly could by her encouragement, openness and love.

Just think of the impact we could have if every single Chris-tian had this attitude and determination to allow the example of our lives to do more "witnessing" than our mouths. Just by helping out another mum at our child's preschool, by reaching out to that person who seems like an outcast in our neighborhood, by letting someone know we are praying for him or her, or by giving a sincere compliment to an acquaintance, we can show the goodness and devotion of God without ever having to preach a word. In the words attributed to St. Francis of Assisi, "Preach the gospel at all times. If necessary, use words."

Selah

- Describe the ways in which your everyday life effective-ly preaches the gospel.

- Think about some people in your life today. Twenty-five years from now, what do you think they will say about the impact you had on their lives?

- If your life were a sermon, what would be the title of your message?

BE: RESPONSIBLE

*We must never shy away from the proclamation of the gospel
of Jesus Christ, "for it is the power of God to salvation for
everyone who believes" (Rom. 1:16).*

Don't you hate it when you look in the mirror and you notice a
huge piece of spinach between your teeth—and you ate that
spinach at lunch *five hours ago*?

You begin to mentally retrace your steps over the last few
hours, and you think of all the people you know must have seen
the garish thing and didn't say a word! The client with whom you
were trying to close the deal, your boss, your coworker in the adja-
cent cubicle . . . You suddenly realize that the guy at the espresso
stand was not smiling at you because he thought you were cute; he
was giggling about the head of spinach lodged between your teeth.
Why didn't anyone tell me about that?! you wonder.

Carrying spinach around in your teeth isn't necessarily life-
threatening (unless you are single), and the result of this lack of eti-
quette is usually nothing more than a few moments of embarrass-
ment. But what if you were walking with a friend, not paying attention to where you were going, both laughing about the movie you
just saw, and *BAM!*—you walked straight into a pole! Your friend

had delicately walked around it but had failed to point it out to you. As soon as you pick yourself up off the side of the road, first thing you would say is, "Why didn't you warn me about that?!"

Let's take it up a notch. You and a friend are at the playground with your children. One of your own children needs your attention, so you kindly ask your friend to watch your eldest child. As she is "watching" little Johnny, he wanders out into the street to pick up a penny. From across the park, you look up to see a truck flying down the street in the direction of your son. As you sprint to save him, I am sure one of your thoughts is, *Why didn't she do something about that?!*

There is a lost, broken and hurting world all around us, and we have the answer in Jesus. If we, the Church, don't speak up and do something about it, then who will? People's eternities are at stake.

Selah

- When was the last time that you introduced someone to Jesus?

- In your world, list tangible examples of what it means to (1) preach the gospel to the poor, (2) heal the broken-hearted, (3) proclaim liberty to the captives, (4) restore the blind, and (5) set the oppressed free.

- Have you made it your personal responsibility to live out these works of mercy in your own world? If not, resolve today to start living out the gospel of Christ.

BE: VOCAL

When we truly love our neighbor as we love ourselves, we cannot help but proclaim this life-saving Word to them.

Remember in junior high school when the girls used to doodle all over their notebooks, drawing huge hearts with their initials and some boy's initials inside the heart? Invariably there would always be a "TLA" nearby, meaning "True Love Always!" Or if the girl was not interested in boys yet, she would have her name plus her best friend's name with a big "BFF" next to it, meaning "Best Friends Forever!" In our youth, we were just beginning to understand the joy of close friendships, and we wanted to make sure we let everyone know about it.

When Nick and I started dating and falling in love, I was past the stage of doodling "Mrs. Christine Caine" on every available scrap of paper, but I must admit that I did have to make an effort to not make Nick the center of every conversation. The trust, love, laughter and closeness were things that were so new and I was so happy about our relationship that I sometimes just couldn't help myself. And once we got married and had children, all restraint was thrown out the window! I cannot help talking about my loving husband and my beautiful princesses (no surprise to those of you reading this book)! And God bless any person I am sitting next to on a plane as I have an entire photo slideshow of my family ready to go on my Blackberry.

When our relationship with Jesus is fresh and passionate, it is the same way. We cannot help but proclaim how much we love Him and how He has changed our lives. Now, I'm not suggesting we plant huge signs in our front yards that say "I Heart Jesus, TLA!" Or "J.C. + Me = BFF!" We simply need to ensure that our conversations with our neighbors leave room for expressing the joy and sense of security that flow from our relationship with Him. When we are in a love affair with Jesus and when we are still in awe of such a wonderful gift as salvation, talking about our faith never feels like a duty or obligation.

Selah

- What is one way that you personally express your love to others?

- Do you find yourself expressing your love for Jesus in the same way that you express your love for people (and vice versa)?

- Read the definition of love in 1 Corinthians 13. Select three of these characteristics of love that you can work on developing during the next week.

- Think of one person in your world whom you would characterize as "loving." Then explain why you attribute that quality to this person.

BE: INTERRUPTIBLE

*People are not an interruption in our lives—
they are why we're here.*

You know those days when you have 14 things to accomplish by that evening, and in order to succeed, you plan every minute? I recently had one of those, and I had every detail perfectly mapped out. There was no room in the schedule for mistakes or interruptions, but I was confident that I could overcome anything that might attempt to thwart my day.

I finished feeding both girls and began the task of getting everyone loaded into the car. In the bustle of activity, I must have swung poor Sophia around too many times because she proceeded to spit up a small portion of her breakfast on my shirt. *My plan!* I thought, *I'll have to clean that off as I'm driving.* I packed the girls and began my journey only a few minutes late. I wasn't worried about that, though, because I could shave off a few minutes at Catherine's parent-teacher meeting by talking really fast.

I got Sophia to the sitter and Catherine to school—and, sure enough, I was able to make up some time with my lightning-fast Grecian speaking ability. Next, I headed to the super-market for some dinner ingredients before my big meeting started. I almost lost my Christianity standing behind a woman who clearly had *three times* the item limit for the express check-out line. Again, I was behind on my plan.

As I was rushing out with my groceries, I noticed a woman with a double stroller struggling to get into the bathroom. *Wow, twins,* I marveled. *She's never going to fit in that tiny stall. I hope some-one helps her.*

To my surprise, the Holy Spirit prompted, "Why don't *you* help her?"

Then I almost laughed aloud at the notion. *My plan!* I replied, *I couldn't possibly stop right now.*

I don't think He heard me because He repeated Himself.

Seriously, I argued, *I can't right now. God, You know everybody— You have someone else do it.*

At that point, I started to think God needed a hearing aid because He repeated Himself again!

Eventually I relented and walked over to the woman and asked if I could help. To my surprise, she burst into tears. Embarrassed, she tried to control herself as she explained that her husband had just left her and her newborn twins. She had no idea how she was going to make it, and all she wanted to do was go to the bathroom without a struggle!

Suddenly, my "plan" didn't seem so important. I sat and talked to this woman and helped connect her with a pastor for counseling and support, and then I thanked God for the inter-ruption and for using me (albeit with a lot of coercing) to make a difference in the life of a hurting person.

Selah

• When you have a plan, how hard does God have to work at getting you to change it?

• Can you think of a time when you allowed the Holy Spirit to "interrupt" you so that you could help someone else? What was the result of your obedience?

• Make some time to people watch. Be on the lookout for opportunities to help others—opportunities that you would normally miss because you are usually so focused on your own agenda.

• What changes would you need to make in your life in order to allow God room to interrupt you?

• Read Mark 5:21-42. What happened when Jesus allowed Jairus to interrupt His meeting?

BE: A CHRISTIAN

*You and me, a strong army of men and women, refusing to
simply act like a Christian, but determined to be one.*

At the very beginning of this devotional section, I talked about
how a *Selah* is a time to stop and take a moment to reflect on
what has just been said. It's a time to allow a thought or a concept to sink down deep into your heart. For this final *Selah*, let's
visualize what our world would look like if every Christian
decided to simply *be* a Christian.

Imagine if every single person who proclaimed themselves to
be Christian (and there are billions of us) spent every day loving
God with all their heart, all their soul and all their mind, and if
every single one loved their neighbor as themselves. What if this
love was the motivating factor behind every prayer we prayed,
every word we uttered, every interaction we had, every thought
we thought and every action we took? Think of the tremendous
affect we would have on our towns, cities and nations.

One by one, with arms linked, we would form an undeni-
ably strong army whose voice could not be ignored. Our presence would impact our culture and government. We would be
a voice for the poor, marginalized and depressed, righting

wrongs and fighting injustice. We would revolutionize the face of our media, education system, economy and environment. We would see the lost come home, eager to taste for themselves the goodness of God they have seen in the Christians around them. *Selah*.

I realize this might sound a bit utopian, but it is entirely possible. We actually have the potential within us to shape this planet! It simply begins with a choice to give up our roles as Christians and to decide to truly *be* one from the core of who we are. It starts with you and me living our lives as authentic Christians.

There are many mind-sets and opinions about what a Christian really is, but we must ensure that we always come back to the Word of God as our benchmark for what it means to be one. I ended each *Selah* with questions for further reflection so that you can consider your own spiritual journey and therefore be empowered to explain to others what being a Christian really means.

Maybe after reading this book, you need to put it down and focus for a bit on a particular core muscle. Maybe you just need to be more aware of the impact your life is already making so that your witness can have an even greater influence, or maybe you just need to go sit on a rock with God and just *be* for a while. Regardless of what you do when you shut this book, my prayer is that you allow the heart of this message to sink in and that your life soon bears the fruit of it.

Being a Christian is not something we can master and then move beyond. It is a daily choice and a determination. It is something we can forever be improving on, learning from and sharing with others. It's a journey. It's an adventure!

I'm going to leave you with a decision to make. You can choose to put this book down and mark it off as another accomplished read, or you can determine to challenge yourself daily in your normal, everyday life—through trials and success—asking yourself this question:

Am I just acting like a Christian, or am I truly being one?

ACKNOWLEDGMENTS

My sincere and heartfelt thanks to:

My amazing husband, Nick. I love you so much and thank God every day of my life that He has given you to me. You release me to enter into the "book bubble," and fill in all the gaps that enable our life to continue.

My beautiful daughters, Catherine Bobbie and Sophia Joyce Grace, for being patient with Mummy and my comic relief.

My senior pastors, Brian and Bobbie Houston, who have been a consistent example of what it is to be a true Christian. I value your love, support and friendship, and look forward to the journey ahead.

Dave and Joyce Meyer, your lives are such a source of inspiration to me. You are the real deal and wonderful role models of what it is to be a Christian. Thank you for believing in me and encouraging me to continue to develop the inner life.

Molly Venzke and Annie Dollarhide, words cannot express my gratitude for your total commitment to this project. Without you it would not be what it is.

Sarah, Ashley and the whole E & E team for loving my girls, jumping on the trampoline, swinging on the swings and reading *Cinderella* (again!) so that I could write.

Natalie Laborde, Maria Ieroianni, James Inglis and Maree Chapman, your input and assistance with the editing process is very much appreciated.

To Kim Bangs and the team at Regal, thank you for believing in me and the message of this book, for your patience, support, flexibility and encouragement. It has been a privilege working with you.

ABOUT THE AUTHOR

A sought-after speaker around the world, Christine Caine is a gifted communicator with a heart for reaching the lost and helping people unlock their God-given potential.

She is known for her "tell it like it is," passionate and humorous way of communicating. Together with her husband, Nick, Christine is part of the leadership team at Hillsong Church in Sydney, Australia, as well as a director of Equip & Empower Ministries. Their key missions focus is Project Europe, a church-planting and leadership-development initiative throughout Europe.

She lives her life to the *full* as a wife, a mother of two beautiful daughters, a teacher, a preacher and an author. When the family isn't changing the world on the road, they make their home in Sydney, Australia.

Other books by Christine Caine include *A Life Unleashed* and *Youth Ministry—Principles for the 21st Century*.

www.chriscaine.com
www.equipandempower.org

OTHER BOOKS BY CHRISTINE CAINE

A Life Unleashed

In this book Christine paints an inspiring and often hilarious picture of what it takes to overcome the obstacles in life, inorder to give birth to your dreams.

With thought-provoking questions and fresh insight, Christine not only leads you to a better understanding of God's Word, but through her powerful life story she also inspires you to live a life unleashed!

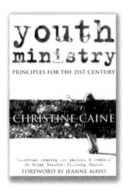

Youth Ministry: Principles for the 21st Century

In our postmodern 21st century, defined by compromise and relativism, we need radical leaders that will adhere to Biblical values, have a holistic approach to youth ministry, champion the cause of the local church and believe that the Gospel works.

This book is perfect for youth pastors, and leaders in your church!

For more information about resource from Christine Caine:

www.equipandempower.org

www.chriscaine.com

PO Box 7820 Baulkham Hills BC

NSW 2153 Australia

Ph: +61 2 9659 5400 Fax: +61 2 9659 6499